I0142856

Testimonials

You're Not Broken: Shifting from Fear & Anxiety to Strength & Empowerment is a beautiful, heartfelt work. I am grateful for the courage and strength the women have shown to willingly share their personal stories of trauma and abuse that resonate with many of us as we continue on our own healing journeys. Her book reminds us that we are not stuck and trapped in our pain and anxieties forever, and that healing is possible for all of us. You can tell that Cindy genuinely, deeply cares about helping people through their pain and journey in healing. There are so many women that will benefit from reading this, seeing that it's okay to feel your feelings and move through them, all while remembering there is hope for you yet for a happier, more empowered life.

~Jenn

The women's personal stories deeply resonated with me. I feel connected to them, and that I'm not alone in my own process. I clearly began to see how my own childhood trauma has directly affected my stuck patterns and relationship problems. After reading, I have renewed hope and motivation to be true to myself, stop judging myself and create the life I want. This book was easy to read, and the points are well driven!

~Jody

I really loved this very easy to read work. The women's real-life stories gave me the courage to speak up for myself and to realize, despite how broken my past has caused me to feel, that I am worthy of a happy life! This book will support any woman to create better relationships, more happiness and peace. For the first time, I feel that I fully understand my need for boundary setting, and I have found my "No." I have renewed self-confidence and actually feel ok to enjoy happiness that I haven't felt since being a child. The journal prompts at the end of each chapter, have compelled me to make the changes necessary to live life on my terms.

~Kate

You're NOT BROKEN

Shifting from Fear and Anxiety to

Strength & Empowerment

Cindy Jesse LISW, MSW

Copyright © 2021 Cindy Jesse

All rights reserved. No part of this book may be used or reproduced by any means, graphic, electronic, or mechanical, including photocopying, recording, taping or by any information storage retrieval system without the written permission of the publisher except in the case of brief quotations.

Inspired Press Publisher
1333 Chelsea Court
Morrow, OH 45152
www.inspiredpresspublisher.com
513-256-1792

ISBN-13: 978-1-7336423-5-4

Library of Congress Control Number: 2021916241

Dedication

This book is dedicated to my husband, Steve, for always cheering me on and tirelessly offering help in any way. You are my lover, my best friend, and life partner! I love you!

Also, to my beautiful children, grandchildren, and future generations to come! Do your work! Keep evolving! Your gifts are beautiful and eternal! Do everything better than we did! I love you forever and always!

Heartfelt THANK YOU's to Kathleen for editing this work; to Dave for coaching me to tell heartfelt, descriptive stories; to Connie and Sharon for reading the first draft and being so honest as I know that wasn't easy; to Jenn, Jody, and Hally for helping in so many ways… reading final drafts, offering encouragement, going over titles and covers. I appreciate all of you and love you so much!

Table of Contents

Introduction

*T*his book is written from the perspective of women young and old who've faced and endured the storms of life that, unfortunately, many females face. Although, overwhelmed at times by feelings that this triumph could never be possible, we've made it through to the other side. We've gone from feeling afraid and anxious to courageously believing that we could be like the strong, soft, yet empowered, beautiful women we admire.

Growing up with mistreatment, including emotional and physical neglect, physical violence, verbal emotional abuse, and/or sexual abuse left us feeling broken, unworthy, lost, stuck, unlovable, and unacceptable. Many times, we faced being mistreated as adults because we lacked boundaries. We became angry, needy, victim-y, people pleasers (and we despise these feelings). We knew we were unhealthy and our true identity got lost just trying to survive traumas, causing us to wonder if we could ever retrieve it. Sometimes, we even felt as though life wasn't worth living anymore. Like, "What's the point?" However, this writing is full of authentic hope for survivors like you and me.

This book provides you with a good mix of professionally expert yet practically helpful ways of healing your emotional life. I share our journey from feeling broken and unworthy to finally finding for the first time, peace and calm. How we realized we are enough. How we began to pay attention to our own emotions for the first time. How we recognized how special we have always been. How we corrected the dysfunctional programs and beliefs in our heads, and for the first time began to feel and act like healthy adults. It's not only possible to achieve, but also so incredible to become your own true self, to love her deeply and to vow to never let her go!

This work has taken me many years to write and finish. I completed the first draft about 5 or 6 years ago which I asked two friends to read. They both kindly and supportively agreed. When I met with them afterward to hear their thoughts, both looked at me with a face that said, "Are you serious?!" Although I met with them separately, their feedback was similar – the book lacked feeling and authenticity. They said the first draft reminded them more of a graduate school textbook! I was stunned, initially. But the more they shared, the more I realized they were 100% right. I was humbled, and realized I initially hid the stories behind psychological theory. I wrapped it all up as a nice, beautiful package with a big bow. When my friends opened it, they found me fake and hidden. Why? I came to realize that while I wanted to believe I had done all my work, I hadn't. I avoided going too deep into my story because some of the content would re-open old wounds and trigger emotions. But instead of immediately diving back into making changes in the book, I hit the pause button to complete deeper self-care work on my personal trauma.

Once I was able to face and heal from it, my passion for the story of this work returned with fierce love and determination. I also worked with a book coach! After three more years of writing and editing, what you're reading now is the result - authentic stories chock full of reality, truth, feelings, and healing. I'm so grateful my friends were honest with me! Authentic, true friends are worth more than anything this world offers.

My dream is that this work serves women everywhere who are stuck, feeling broken, and feeling like they could use some encouragement to keep hoping, healing, and find lasting peace and great joy! I'm a strong advocate for helping women who've been victims of any kind of sexual assault, to get to know, take back and own their power!

To this date, I've worked as a therapist at an agency for four years followed by my current private practice for a little over 12 years. I love my work! I get up every day and feel incredibly lucky and grateful to do this very unique, divinely inspired work. This feels like more of a calling than a job. I have met and worked with some of the most amazing souls! Several of them were courageously willing to let me share part of their stories with you so you could see the emotional healing that happened in their lives as they shifted from being stuck in fear and anxiety to living their best lives with strength and empowerment. Many of them went on to become entrepreneurs. For some reason, many women who desire to start businesses often call me to work with them. While building my practice, I realized I have a naturally innate knowledge for business acumen, so I began helping clients gain the confidence needed to take the risks. I love walking along side my clients as they realize their lifelong dreams of becoming entrepreneurs!

May the stories in _You're Not Broken: Shifting from Fear and Anxiety to Strength and Empowerment_, resonate with you and give you courage for your own path to strength and empowerment. Sending lots of LOVE your way!

Cindy Jesse
COACHING

TOOLS FOR YOUR EMPOWERMENT

My vision for empowering women has always been more than these pages. Below are tools that will help strengthen and empower you.

www.cindyjessecourses.com
Visit www.cindyjessecourses.com to find free meditations, blogs and courses as well as for-purchase courses for your personal growth and enjoyment.

www.cindyjesse.com
Visit www.cindyjesse.com if you'd like to schedule a 1-on-1 appointment when life feels unmanageable. You can experience the peace, happiness and self-confidence you deserve.

Become a member of my free Facebook Group (Private) named, **Encouragement and Empowerment for Empathic Women**. This group is for women who are empaths and want to be part of a group that encourages them and lets them know they are not alone. There are many of us and we are intuitive, sensitive and have beautiful gifts to celebrate and share!

https://www.facebook.com/groups/381765266826016/

Chapter 1

See Your Worth, Know That You Matter

My client: Meghan's story:

Our three-bedroom, one story house was anything but average. The little front yard was perfectly manicured, from green lawn to colorful landscaping, with a scalloped white fence protecting a proud display of perennial shrubs and seasonal fragrant flowers. This yard was a reflection of my dad. He liked all things perfect. Everything he did was razor-sharp as he eyeballed it precisely. I remember admiring that about him. However, even in my 4-year-old world, I felt deep inside that I wouldn't, I couldn't, measure up. I found my daddy, then, to be the smartest, tallest, strongest, most interesting man. I knew deep inside he knew anything there was to know about everything. He was almost like a God to me. Back then, my dad was trying to better our lives as he worked hard at a manufacturing factory during the day and took evening classes at the local community college at night. He was gone much of our waking hours.

I remember one morning leaning on the front screen door with my nose and forehead on the glass until the cold air on the other side caused me to wince and take a few steps back. I noticed the neighbors' dads leaving for work, and the moms and kids pressed up against their screen doors waving goodbye. I wondered why my mom, my little sister, and I didn't stand at the door and wave goodbye. "Poor daddy." I thought, "We don't stand at the door and wave goodbye when he leaves."

He hadn't come out from his shower to leave for work yet and when he reached the kitchen, he called my name. There was something so exciting to me when my dad, who didn't say much normally, called my name. He put his hands under my arms as he lifted my little body up onto the sturdy kitchen table and sat me down, his hands straightening my legs out perfectly. Dad always made sure whatever he was writing or working with was straight, well-organized, perfect. I looked at my two little feet out in front of me as my dad bent over to be face-to-face with me. He looked me straight in the eyes. I knew when he looked at me straight in the eyes something important was coming. I remember feeling kind of giddy to feel so important to him and to be, in this moment in time, the center of his attention. This man was my world, and I loved him deeply by the age of four. I remember wiggling my little padded butt on the table in anticipation of what he was going to say. Would he say, "We're going to grandma's house for dinner tonight?", or maybe, "We have company coming!" His stern face and piercingly bold blue eyes told me that what he was going to say was serious.

At that moment, I smelled burned coffee wafting from the coffee pot. I liked that smell. It was familiar. Little light flickers from the chandelier over my head danced on his face and on my legs. Daddy always made sure we had what we needed, and now he's about to tell *me* something very important. He leaned over and said,

"Meghan, I need you to be responsible, honey. Mom isn't feeling well and she needs you to help her. Don't mess up the house and help take care of Jenny." My little toddler heart would have moved a mountain if my dad had asked me! I thought the world of my dad, as I think most little girls do. I wanted to do anything that pleased him or made him smile at me. "Okay, I will, Daddy!" I didn't even ask what the word "responsible" meant because I didn't want to interrupt that moment between us, and I would never want him to think of me as stupid. Dad didn't like stupid people. They mostly "ticked him off," as I'd heard him say many times. Dad picked me up again from under my arms and put me down from the table, grabbed his keys from the counter, and headed out the front door.

My dad had no idea the burden he was placing on my little 4-year-old mind and body. I know if he'd known how much this would change me, he wouldn't have said it. Basically, he was telling me, "You're alone, and I'm sorry. Your mother is tired (passed out), and you have to be much older than you are, and you have to take care of adult things you really don't understand yet."

After I listened to his car drive away, the quiet morning and lingering silence became piercing. I felt alone as I stood looking around the barely day-lit living room. It was a beautiful room. Green and blue flowered chairs and a big blue couch to match, tables with pretty lamps, the statue of a pretty woman's shoulders and head, curtains that hung softly. If someone were to walk into our house, they would notice it was perfectly decorated and properly maintained. There were two pictures of ladies leaning against musical instruments hanging on the wall. When I remember the ladies' faces, they were strangely sultry. However, in my child's mind, I saw them as naughty, mysterious and fun. "Who were these mysterious women? Did we know them?" I grinned.

The silence that morning was broken by a cry coming from down the hallway. I realized my baby sister, Jenny, was finally awake. I skipped down the textured, green-carpeted hall, brushing the hallway walls with my fingertips. I opened bedroom door, and there was my little, baby sister. She was in a beautiful, lacy room wearing scalloped pink polka-dotted pajamas, sitting behind the spindles of her baby bed, finger in her mouth. She was crying. The moment Jenny spotted me, she stopped crying for a few seconds and grinned, tears twinkling in her little blue eyes. She loved me and was happy to see me, which felt so warm to me. I was Jenny's big sister and I felt motherly toward her. As I closed the door behind me, she proceeded to scream as she held her hand to her mouth. I put my hands in through the spindles to tickle her and play with her. I began thinking that I should go wake up Mom because no matter what I did, Jenny didn't stop crying. "Maybe she's hungry," I thought. I gently spoke, "I'll be right back, Jenny! I promise." This didn't comfort her. She began screaming and stood in her bed and reached up to the top of the railing, gripping it hard, while screaming even louder. I walked out of Jenny's room, my little heart breaking because I didn't want to leave her. I re-opened her door and, in a soft baby voice, I said, "I will be right back and bring Mommy, okay?" She didn't buy it.

I walked across the green, textured carpeting to my mom's bedroom. "Mom, wake up!" She rolled over and opened one eye for a split second, long enough to see me, and sighed as she rolled over, mumbling something. It seemed like something was wrong, like she was tired or paralyzed. This wasn't unusual for my mom, so I wasn't alarmed. I tried to understand what she was mumbling, and I again said, "Mom, wake up! Jenny's ready for breakfast." I could tell by her slight grimace and painful sigh that she wanted me to stop trying to wake her. I wandered toward the door, taking one quick glance back, hoping with everything in me that she was sitting up and getting her house slippers on, inspired to make oatmeal as she did some mornings. But she wasn't moving. The only thing I knew to do was go back to Jenny's room.

I walked back into Jenny's room. She was crying hysterically. I started to feel really scared and seriously thought about crying myself. Just then, I remembered that Daddy was counting on me. I attempted to lift Jenny out of her baby crib but I wasn't strong enough. I had to figure this out. Jenny was hungry and crying and I couldn't get her out of bed. The only thing I knew to do was to get into the bed with her. I climbed and climbed and shimmied until, finally, I was in! She kept crying even though I was in there with her, holding her like I would hold one of my doll babies. I knew she was hungry so I managed to climb back out of her bed, reassuring her again in that soft little baby voice, that I would be back. Her screams were shrill and went right up my spine. I noticed tears dropping from my cheek. I wiped them away. That was the moment I knew I was all alone. As I wiped my tears off of my face, I somehow knew I would be wiping away my feelings for many years. If I felt my feelings, I'd be in a heap on the floor next to Jenny's bed. Then who would take care of her?

I made my way down the hall to the tidy kitchen. The bright morning sun was peering through the window, bouncing onto the almond green stove and then onto my face. I moved out of the sun's rays so that I could see the cabinets. I spotted the cabinet where I knew there was a jar of peanut butter, on the top shelf next to the refrigerator. I tried climbing up the fridge by the handle, but that only opened the refrigerator door and shook the bottles inside.

I decided to move one of our metal and plastic, cushioned chairs over in front of the cabinet. I climbed up onto the chair and then onto the counter and very carefully, stood up on the counter to reach the top shelf. I was standing on the counter with peanut butter in my hands but as I looked down at how far away the linoleum flowered floor was, I began to feel frightened. Very slowly, I sat on the counter and then jumped to the chair and finally, I was back on the floor. I walked down the hallway with a jar of Skippy creamy peanut butter, got into Jenny's bed, opened the peanut butter, and began to scoop it out with my finger. I began feeding her little bits of peanut butter from my finger. She stopped crying and soon fell back to sleep.

I remember coming up to the side of my mom's bed again, stroking her hair and begging her to get up because it was so very quiet in the house. I desperately hoped she would realize I was there and that I needed her to get out of bed to be with my little sister and me. Mom just seemed very, very sleepy and annoyed. I left the room, shut her door quietly and turned on the television to channel 19, to watch morning cartoons.

In my little mind's eye, I didn't understand why there seemed to be a dark cloud over our small, perfectly manicured, perfectly furnished house. I didn't know why my mom was so sleepy, that many mornings and afternoons she would lay passed out in her bed.

As an adult, I began to explore the "whys" of my childhood and realized Mom was taking prescription valium, a drug that primary care physicians regularly prescribed for women in the 1970's. My mom was escaping, as best she could, her own memories of growing up too fast, of her own abuse. Finally, it all soon made sense to me, but my old fear and anxiety didn't budge.

Dad was asking me, a four-year-old, to be all grown-up those mornings. He never would have asked if he'd known the weight of what he was placing on me. This pressure followed me through my teen years and into adulthood. I was being served notice on that bright summer morning that I was on my own, that he had to leave all day, that Mom was over and out, and that I was alone. I didn't realize it then, but when I look back at that beautiful, little girl, with white shiny hair, big blue eyes, and little white gym shoes, she was physically on her own at times; she was emotionally on her own always. No one was going to pad her falls, wipe her nose, hug her when she fell. No one was going to hug and kiss her out of the blue and say, "I love you!" She was on her own and she would be handling anything that came her way throughout elementary school, middle school, high school and into adulthood.

The End of Meghan's Story

Many of us, at a young age, experienced absent or distant parents, whether they left us or were alcoholics, drug addicts, or battling other addictions. At some point, the child who lives in a home like this one, realizes that she is basically on her own. The child realizes that things are best when she is not in the way or is "seen but not heard," as the saying goes. As children, we may become overly responsible, always productive, trying to be perfect, people-pleasers. Ultimately, by the age of thirty-something, we are dead inside.

My own search for approval and my striving to be perfect, productive and people-pleasing, led me to feeling frustrated, dead inside, and desperate for a way out.

While cleaning up breakfast dishes one rainy morning, I was listening to a psychology call-in show in my own well-appointed kitchen. I stopped in my tracks as a defeated woman's words pierced my heart. The woman was sobbing. Maybe you've heard this kind of cry, the kind that is broken by quick, labored, "I can barely catch my breath to speak," breaths. She said, "I'm at the end of my rope.

I have no more left to give." She choked back her raging tears and continued, "I feel so stuck. I hate my life. My mom calls me on the phone every morning and complains about her life, her unhappy marriage to my dad, and then, she never fails to remind me where I'm sucking at life, too. My husband works 24/7 and says it's just his strong work ethic. He doesn't have time for the kids or me. And the kids," she gulped back the tears, "need constant attention. Every day is the same - taking care of the kids, changing diapers, cleaning up their messes, cooking, and staring at the mountains of laundry. I work so hard to stay ahead, and yet I still feel so guilty and miserable most of the time. Sometimes I wonder: 'Is this it? Is this all my life is going to be? Am I the only one who feels this lost and stuck and crazy?'" As I loaded the last cereal spoon into the dishwasher, my eyes welled up. That woman's pain resonated with me.

I began to chime in with her, "Yeah! Is this it? Constant messes to clean up, rivers of milk and Cheerios spreading across the tile every morning, morning after morning, and endless mountains of laundry? Will I be sixty years old one day, whining to my beautiful daughter about my own crappy life, complaining about her daddy and saying things that make her feel inadequate?" Just then, my eyes wandered over to my little girl, Elise, sitting in her chair at the kitchen table, smiling, wearing her pink and green Little Mermaid nightgown, red-painted toes dangling from her chair, finishing up her Breakfast of Champions, while she perused the cereal box cartoons. She caught my eyes looking her way, and as she tilted her head to one side, smiled sweetly. "No way," I thought, deep inside.

Looking at her eternal blue eyes and longer-than-life lashes, I knew that I didn't want to go through my life being angry and unhappy. My son, Matthew, had finished with his cereal and, in typical fashion, was creating his next new book, complete with illustrations.

His brown eyes so sweet; and my baby, Steven, was sitting in his Batman cape in the high chair, singing songs from Sunday school.

As I looked at these three, I knew then that I didn't want my children to grow up with a mom like me. I wanted to be one of those extraordinary women, like the speakers I'd seen at the weekend women's conferences. Those speakers were confident, knew where they're going, and seemed to live their lives to the fullest! That's what I wanted in my vision of the future for myself, but that day, most days, I just couldn't be that. I could never imagine being confident. When I looked at my future, I didn't like what I saw.

I listened to several women ask questions of the psychologists' panel that day. That particular woman's words seemed to go through me. I felt like she could read my thoughts. Have you ever felt like someone was speaking to you and able to see inside you and know your thoughts? Like the caller, I felt stuck, anxious, depressed, and paralyzed.

A desperate feeling rose up in me later that afternoon, kind of like an "ah-ha" moment. No! No, I refuse to believe that this is how it has to be! I refuse to stay stuck in this place. There's got to be more to this life. I have to be worth more than this, and if I'm not, what's the point? What if I'm not worth more than being a doormat? Am I destined to be the responsible one, the one who has to be there for everyone when they need me and then, deep down, resent them? I thought about my precious little girl, and said to myself, "Is that what

I want for her?" The very thought of it made me sick to my stomach, but even then, I didn't see a way to change.

That day, I called a therapist from the show's list, and while on hold, I began to think, "What am I doing? No one I know goes to therapy. Don't you have to be crazy to go to therapy?"

But then, I thought, "Maybe I am crazy. It probably costs a lot of money." The receptionist answered and I made an appointment to see Dr. Meg.

The day of that appointment came, much to my chagrin. I woke up feeling excited and, at the same time, regretted having made the appointment. I thought about canceling the appointment, but, to my surprise, Dr. Meg was kind and warm. She took me back to her small office and we sat down to talk. I felt, for the first time in my life, someone was hearing me. I wasn't invisible. Dr. Meg was so present with me in those sessions. I'd never experienced a conversation that was focused only on me, with someone listening only to me, with someone so *there* for me.

There were times I considered skipping my next appointment because things became so real in those moments in her office. Maybe I could continue to deny how bad my life felt. Nevertheless, I went to sessions with Dr. Meg every week. I wrote my feelings down in my journal as she asked, read the books she suggested, and went to group therapy. I was genuinely beginning to take action for myself, treating myself like I mattered. I began to feel there may be hope for me and for my life for the first time. I even felt some occasional glimpses of happiness.

I began to understand that the patterns I had in my life were a direct result of not feeling my feelings. I started to see that I had unresolved, unprocessed feelings from the years and years of events in my life. They were patterns of feeling like I was different from other people, like I didn't fit in, feeling less than others, and feeling like everyone except me got the memo on life. These "stuffed-down for years" feelings were following me into my adult life and making me feel depressed, anxious and, worst of all, bitter.

I felt it most when I would agree to do something I didn't want to do. Like the time I agreed at 10:00 pm to bake 48 cupcakes by the next morning for one of my kid's preschool classes; or having sex when I was tired of feeling disconnected from my husband; or babysitting someone's kids after I'd watched them two other days that same week; or sitting on the phone for an hour while someone else droned on and on about her life. I felt resentful! I would isolate myself and try to shut out the world. I was blaming everyone else. I'd start to feel like a victim. "Poor me! Can't these people see how hard I am working for them? Don't they see how hard doing all their stuff is on me? Do they appreciate anything I do for them?" I had a giant pity party. Have you ever felt like this?

I realized that my anxiety and depression and feeling stuck were not enemies trying to ruin my life, or even "disorders" I needed to medicate. They actually were my friends, and they were whisper-ing, "Stop putting yourself last. Stop taking care of everyone and every-thing but yourself. Stop being a doormat! You matter, too." When I look back and imagine myself in that kitchen on that day, feeling so worthless and having so little hope, compassion floods my heart for that young mother of three, and for all other women over the years who have silenced their voices as they felt they didn't matter.

Unless I began to take responsibility for my own dysfunction, I was going to carry it into future generations, like a spreading cancer.

My only close-up experience with cancer involved my friend, Sue. She had breast cancer. I sat beside her in this cold room with a drip of poison medicine going into her body that I prayed would kill the cancer that was killing her. If you've never been, it feels like this person, this person who is so important to you, is on a gaming table just waiting for her number to come up. I'm sure many of you have either been the patient in that dreaded chair with that dreaded drip, or the friend sitting with your loved one while he or she gets sicker and sicker from the poison that drips in to fight the nasty cells. It's brutal to deal with cancer. I compare, with deep respect, the pain of past abuse and trauma to cancer - it needs to be squashed or it will eventually kill you. Like chemo, therapy is a necessary healing process and may save your life, but it's very painful and you are pretty sure you might die.

As you will read in the ensuing chapters, I did climb out of the morass and became a therapist. Over my past 10 years as a therapist, I've come to realize that many of us, from childhood to adulthood, have experienced some type of trauma, or multiple traumas, during our lifetime. The latest statistics for sexual abuse for women, are 1 in 4. The gap seems to be shrinking as women are feeling safer to tell their stories. I talk to woman after woman, day after day, young and old, who have experienced **some type of abuse or assault – sexual, verbal, mental, spiritual, physical and/or religious.** It's astounding to me how common these abuses are today, notwithstanding how openly abuse is talked about these days. My personal story of becoming a co-dependent doormat is just one of many. I talk to women everyday who have become silent and have been made smaller by the abuse they experienced.

The good news is that it's definitely possible to heal and become exactly who you were born to be before the abuse changed you. I believe every person born on this planet has a purpose and the needed gifts to fulfill that purpose, but as it unfolds through layers of healing, most people don't realize this about themselves.

Many of us, myself-included for many years, became numb, even dead inside, as a result of abuse. Many of us decide, unknowingly and without a basis in fact, that we deserved the abuse we got and that there was something wrong with us. We believed we were destined to be small, hidden, quiet and invisible. It's possible to discover who you were before the abuse or traumatic event, before being bullied at school, before being bullied by your friend group, or before any other kind of trauma you experienced that made you into an angry, people-pleasing, doormat. I didn't have to stay stuck in that quagmire and neither do you! I began to take off the layered capes of shame and responsibility that were unintentionally thrust onto me over the years.

For me to heal and to recover from my past, I realized I needed to become a student of myself. I had to dig deep if I was going to get to know me. I was so disconnected from myself because for so many years I was staying busy or drinking or numbing out on TV or food to make me forget the abuse. Some of those memories I buried so deep that they were lost inside me, wreaking havoc I could never have imagined. I had to go to therapy, read books, ask for help and put into practice what I learned. I had to put hours into this type of self-care. I slowly began to trust that the Universe had my back. Even more slowly, I learned to trust some people and started to believe that, maybe, life really could be worth living.

Have you ever had a dream and, upon waking, been left with intrigue and wonder about it? What does it mean? Why did I dream that? This happened to me in therapy, frequently. I was getting into bed after my Epsom salt/lavender bath to read a book the evening following one such dream. The dream kept coming back to me. I thought to myself, "Because this dream continues to come up, maybe there's a message in it." Because the dream intrigued me so, and because I was too tired to try to figure it out, I wrote it down in my journal so I could take a look at it the following morning.

Here's what I wrote in my journal:

"I had a dream I was in a nursery or daycare-type room, and there were several kids playing together. The kids were doing what kids do, wrestling, running around, yelling, laughing, and throwing toys. I noticed one little girl she was about 3-4 years old. She was beautiful and delicate; however, her neck was unstable like a newborn's, and her head flopped all over. It looked painful. I also noticed she was missing one eye. I sensed she was very vulnerable. I instantly felt deep compassion for this little girl. She needed someone to care for her tenderly. I picked her up and held her close, and with one hand, I held her little head steady, safe on my chest. As I was feeling sure that she was safe from the crowd of kids playing and roughhousing, a woman came into the room. She was the teacher. She was brash, harsh, and rough. This woman didn't seem to care that the little girl was fragile and needed tenderness. She ordered me to put the little girl back down into the crowd of kids playing. The little girl's head began to flop around again, and she was being trampled by the other kids playing.

As I was writing this dream in my journal, I slowly began to understand it. I realized all three characters in the dream, the little girl, the harsh teacher, and the compassionate character were all parts of me.

I became aware that the dream was meant to show me the different ways I respond to myself. Sometimes I need to be held tenderly, gently and with compassion, when I'm feeling vulnerable, unsteady and beat up. Other times, I am the teacher in the dream. Instead of being compassionate and kind, I beat myself up. I am harsh, demanding and judgmental. I tell myself, "Get it together! Pull yourself up and stop screwing up!" I tell myself to "grow up, stop whining, and stop being stupid." This Is definitely not helpful, but it has become a habit.

Since I've been working on learning to have compassion for myself and to love myself, I've been getting better at catching myself when I'm being the harsh teacher and allow myself instead to be the compassionate helper. When I feel overwhelmed and stressed, and when I feel like I'm screwing everything up, I work on being kind and gentle with myself. I am learning to give myself what I need instead of what I feel I deserve. I take a warm bath with candles, spa music, Epsom salt, and drops of lavender oil. I treat myself like I would treat one of my dear friends if she came to me feeling overwhelmed and beat up from life. Jesus said, "Love your neighbor as yourself." If I "loved" my friends like I sometimes "love" myself, I wouldn't have any friends. I can be a real "mean girl" to myself. I am not a dream expert, but meditating on my own dreams gives me great messages, and I am, I'm happy to say, *becoming* an expert in *me*.

Have you ever felt like something deep inside you was trying to send a message to you? I have. It's a quiet voice, not an audible one, but more like a "knowing." People have all kinds of names for it, but it's a still, small voice. Some people call it Spirit. It doesn't matter what you call it; we all have that quiet voice inside. It's the voice that wants what's best for you, a voice that is loving and kind.

It's the voice that tells you to give time or money to a great cause or to a person in need, even if that person is you. It's gentle, loving, and wise. When I began to explore the loud, mean voices and also to listen to that deeper, quiet voice, my anxiety and depression began to lift, and I could finally start to imagine hope.

This journey of trying to know myself taught me that the part of me that beats me up, the harsh teacher, she's just doing her job. I call her my "little protector." She is a little, smart, resourceful fireball, who developed inside me at a young age to keep me safe. She is a beast of the most protecting and loving kind. She is a spunky little fighter. She puffs up inside me whenever she senses danger. And, when she senses abandonment or rejection, she makes immediate, quick decisions and plans to take care of me, to make a way for me. She became a part of me and is there to help me. This part of me thought that by yelling at me "to get myself together," she was helping me. So, I wrote the following letter to her and I finally thanked that scrappy little part of me for trying to help me all these years. I told her the adult, healed me, can take it from here.

Dear little protector inside,

"You have been one of the most loyal, loving friends I could have asked for. You puffed up and became invincible as you defended me and looked out for my wellbeing. You became loud and fierce, quick and sharp, and you have become whatever I have needed. You have not only protected me, you also protected the ones I love with your antennae-like intuition and ability to strike at a moment's notice. Remember that time you threatened to single-handedly beat up two well-known, big bullies in high school, in front of a quickly gathering crowd? I had never fought anyone a day in my life. Violence just wasn't my nature. But that day, you rose up to the challenge because of your fierce love and protective feelings for another. You had all the confidence that you could take both of them right then and there! You persevered even as our popular, well-dressed friends stared in disbelief of what was coming out of my mouth. You also developed a really intelligent, manipulative side to you. When I learned early in my life that the truth wasn't regarded by most adults, you diligently came up with a plan to adapt to this non-truth to which adults around you were subscribing. You learned to think up an occasional lie when it was necessary to keep me from harsh punishments for truth-telling.

Thank you for all you've done for me all these years. I want you to know that I will handle things from here. I can handle these things in an adult way. You can rest and trust in me. I'm putting you into retirement. You can relax, or play, or go to sleep if you want, because I will no longer need for you to fight for me. So much love and appreciation, Cindy."

My little protector hasn't gone away completely. She's a part of me. She's there. And there are times she rises up and puts her little hands on her hips, and wields strong words, "kettlebell words" I like to call them, and tries to get me in line by saying, "get yourself together!" However, she's much calmer and much less in charge these days, I'm grateful to say.

Self-compassion was needed when I was looking inside at the little girl part of me, seeing her pain. Dr. Kristen Neff has a helpful website, www.self-compassion.org, where she shares her research on self-compassion and provides exercises to help people understand and to begin having genuine compassion and kindness toward themselves. I used this a great deal when I was trying to become less protective and more able to state my truth, calmly and quietly, while maintaining my strength. I no longer needed to make people see me for who I was. It was no longer important to me. It's no longer my business to know other's opinions of me or what is said about me. I know who I am and that is enough.

I've also learned that when I stop judging myself; when I'm generous and loving towards myself as well as kind to myself (in my selftalk), I truly do matter to myself, genuinely. I don't hold any grudges or anger toward myself. I am my own best friend first. Self-compassion was key to me believing that I matter, and I had to matter to myself to begin to come alive.

I believe the Universe is about truth and authenticity. I believe that because when I judge, hate, and am unkind to myself, I have to fake being non-judgmental, loving, and kind to other people. Did you hear that? I'm only able to be authentically non-judgmental, loving, and kind to all other people if I am genuinely behaving in those ways toward myself. There's a congruency that is real, an unwritten universal law: Hate yourself, you will hate others, too; judge yourself, you'll be judgmental toward others; show compassion and kindness to yourself, you'll be compassionate and kind toward other people. Once I started to practice these things with myself every day, I was sharing that light with others. I was able to open up and realize I had real desires for my life.

My life? Having desires for my life was a little foreign to me. Most of my life was about doing what was expected of me, doing "the right thing," taking care of others' needs and wants. I was a mom and that's pretty standard for moms. When I was people-pleasing, busy doing things for everyone else, I slowly began to die inside. Eventually, there wasn't a trace of "me" to be found. All I could think was that my family needs me, people need me, the community needs me, and the church needs me to do, do, do for them. I was on the back burner. I thought that's the way it was supposed to be - a life of doing and not being. I thought that was the selfless, "Christian" way, the whole "pick up your cross and follow." When I stopped carrying that cross, and started to take a look inside and have compassion and kindness toward myself, my heart's desires rose to the surface and I began to have aspirations. I finally mattered to the most important person I needed to matter to - *me*!

I began to have the desire to go to school, so I started college at the age of thirty-seven. Yes, I was the one asking all the questions and annoying the typical college student, but I was determined to be there for myself, for the first time, and to accomplish the things I wanted to accomplish. Think about the times you've been on an airplane and the flight attendant is standing in the aisle, holding that oxygen mask with the strings, and she instructs you to make sure you put your oxygen mask on first before helping anyone else. Why is putting your mask on first necessary for survival? It's essential to put yours on first because, if you run out of oxygen, you won't be able to help anyone else with his or her oxygen mask. That is a powerful metaphor for those of us who are always taking care of everything and everyone else while neglecting ourselves.

If you don't take care of yourself, if you don't make yourself a priority, you will eventually experience burnout, stress, fatigue, reduced mental effectiveness, health problems, anxiety, depression, frustration and sleep problems, and possibly even death.

If you don't put yourself first on your list, you too, may slowly begin to die. I was stuffing my painful feelings down inside myself day after day; I was letting my voice go more silent, year after year, to the point where I was not only dying inside, I was becoming angry and resentful. This, in turn, caused me to verbally beat myself up and loathe myself more than I had thought possible. It became a vicious cycle of self-hate, self-abuse, and misery. Therapy was one of the first steps for me in helping myself heal from my past abuses, and helping me begin to live again.

I learned many ways to care for myself. I practiced mindfulness, sitting alone in the quiet or with meditation music, and guided meditation. This opened me up to more self-awareness than I'd ever experienced. For me, it's like *experiencing* life instead of just *getting through*. I started to recognize when I was in a sad mood and to ask myself, "why?" For example, I would notice myself being negative. Then, I would sit down with my journal and ask myself, "What is going on here? What am I feeling? What is bothering me beneath the surface?" And just about every time, there would be something that came up inside me; a conversation where I didn't speak up for myself, or maybe someone gave me a nice-nasty comment, or said something that shamed me. Then, I'd have to sit and let the feelings well up inside and allow myself to feel sad and cry or be angry. I had to take time to feel the feelings instead of going to my past coping mechanisms of stuffing the feelings down, and letting my little protector take over. Sometimes, it would be a flash-back of sexual abuse. I'd have to sit with the memories and feel the associated feelings and then, let it go; or, if I needed support, I could process those feelings with my therapist.

I was becoming genuinely hopeful and joyful for the first time in a long time. I saw a life for myself other than being a door-mat, a people-pleaser, a boundary-less bundle of pain hiding from people and life because I had no voice. I had allowed my voice to be stolen years ago by my abusers. I had allowed myself to become reduced to getting through life instead of living it, to dealing with life instead of loving it. That's not *life*.

After some years of continuing my daily practice of asking my heart and higher power for wisdom, I began to feel good most days. I finished school. I began to imagine that I could be the woman I so desperately wanted to be. I could be a woman who put myself on my priority list. You, and only you, are your first hope for healing. And so am I. We have to get to that place where we say, "I matter enough to go tell someone what happened and begin the process of getting better." There truly are so many of us that have similar abuse stories. We are not alone! *We need to know that we matter!* We need to know that what happened to us, mat-ters. When we experience this healing journey, we not only are healing ourselves, we are healing our future children and future generations. That is amazing!

STUDY/DISCUSSION QUESTIONS

- In what ways could you relate to my client, Megan's story?

- When you look back at your childhood, teen years, even some adult years, do you imagine you have some unresolved pain from abuse that's interfering with your current life?

- How's your self-talk? Have you ever committed to observing it for a few days? Do you have a little protector that needs to be retired?

- Do you think maybe you would benefit from a healing process?

- When you examine your current life, are you living as if you matter, or not?

- Do you ever look at other women you admire and wish you could be like them? What would it take to get you to that place where you could admire yourself?

Chapter 2

Everyone Can Heal, Even You!

- Shop online!
- Go to Home Goods and decorate something!
- Drink a couple glasses (or bottle) of wine!
- Call a friend and gossip!
- Watch comedy!
- Watch "reality" TV!
- Read a magazine about celebrity's juicy lives!
- Get busy doing anything to stay busy!

I'd been going to therapy weekly, for a few months, telling my story and my problems to the therapist, and for the first time, beginning to feel my life and dropping my fear of feeling my feelings. Before therapy, I stayed mostly numb so that I wouldn't have to feel. Feeling feelings was scary for me because I hadn't felt anything in many years, probably since I was a child. That's when it happens for most people; when children cry or scream and adults tell them to "stop," to "be quiet." One famous parental saying is, "Stop crying, or I'll give you something to cry about!" It's then we learn to hide our sadness, hide our anger, hide any feelings because it makes adults upset and makes us bad or we get in trouble.

Therapy became painful and somewhat excruciating. The therapy saying is… "it always gets worse before it gets better." I had spent so many years perfecting the art of never feeling anything more than amusement or numbness. That was great! If I began to feel empty or sad, I made fun of something or I could say something witty to make others laugh. I also had that tried-and-true list at the beginning of the chapter, guaranteed to wipe those feelings away or push them down into myself.

The list above was not an exhaustive list, but, you see, I had several ways to stop the sad, painful, hurtful, shameful feelings of the past from bubbling up into my heart and out of my eyes or mouth. Sitting at therapy, in the silence, in the story-telling, in the processing with someone who valued me unconditionally, there came a time that I no longer stuffed those feelings back down inside. They were coming up and out and spilling onto me and staining everything in their path like a bucket of red paint falling from a top shelf onto white carpet. I remember thinking, "What am I doing? Why would anyone want to feel this crap? Why would anyone pay to feel all these sad and angry feelings?" I knew I didn't want to feel this way forever.

One dark day, I realized that I did not want to feel this badly anymore. I did not want to be *here* anymore. I did not want to "face the music," or feelings…so to say. I did not want to look at my past and all the garbage there. I prayed to God, "If you take me now, I won't have to feel these painful, awful feelings." I knew I would never intentionally end my life. I just knew that if I died in my sleep or in a car wreck, I wouldn't have to face these scary, painful feelings or the past. It would just be over. Easy as that! There were three words/names that interrupted my thoughts immediately: Matt, Elise, and Steven, my three children. I knew that if I checked out, they wouldn't have a mom. But then, as the gremlins of shame often do, they stabbed the knife even deeper into my heart and said, "You're a sucky mom anyway; maybe your children would be better off without you in the picture." Shame was like a swirling drain in my head, pulling me further down into the abyss.

I was sobbing in my shame and in my desire to quit life and yet, somewhere inside, I knew I still wanted to be in this life. My husband, Steve, held me and encouraged me and told me that he saw so much good in me. He was the only one of us who could see it at that point. I knew that to heal from my pain, as my therapist had said frequently, I had to "*feel my feelings*" to be freed from the depression. Depression is repressed feelings. Feeling was something I wanted to avoid more than anything. I did not see the point of feeling angry, sad, or hurt; and to be honest, the act of feeling scared me to death! But, people I trusted, people who had been down this road to recovery, were telling me the only way to get better was to let myself finally feel the painful feelings. I decided that, to the best of my ability, I would work to *feel* from now on. There were dark days, I won't lie. Shame was a huge dark cloud over my life and when shame was pouring over me, it took every ounce of strength and courage I had to get out of bed in the morning and face the day and feel. When I look back and remember those days, I feel so grateful that I decided to stick it out in therapy.

As I'm sharing and writing this story, tears are streaming down my cheeks. I think about my children and all the different conversations we've had over the years; I think about their lives and about the milestones they've reached, and I think about how I have loved being a part of their lives. I think about how much I value and love the relationships with my children as they have grown older. I also hear the voices of my many clients, telling me how much my story has helped them to believe they could heal, too; how their lives have changed for the better, and how they have begun to be able to feel their lives and to love themselves. None of this would have been possible if I had chosen to stay in bed and check out. Whatever you've gone through or are facing in your life right now, IT WILL PASS! And you will feel better one day —but only if you do your work.

While in therapy, we find out who we really are and realize who we have tried to be to please everyone else and be "good." Many questions... "What do I believe? Deep down, what are my values, my desires? Did I believe what I was taught in my childhood religion? Did I even know what I believed?" Growing up, I was terrified of a scary, angry, mad, powerful being that lived in the sky that my church and family called God. I imagined God as a very old man with white hair, a white beard and piercing eyes. I imagined his personality like a mean kid with a magnifying glass hovering over me, the little ant, that could be zapped at any moment. This God perpetuated violence and anger and insisted you "toe the line *or else!*" My idea of God back then is certainly not the God, I believe in today.

As I have explored my own spirituality over the years, I've come to know a loving being, full of grace and kindness. As a child, I was taught the only people God approves of are the people who pray this prayer or that prayer, and believe this or that from the Bible, act this way or that, resist this or that. Also, everyone who doesn't do what the church says, are destined to Hell. I remember always having a little pause in my mind when hearing these things. Now I know it was "the knowing." I was done with listening to other people and their interpretations and their versions of God and the Bible. If there was a God, I had to find God on my own terms. I had to get serious and seek God for myself. What I found in my search was a good, kind, loving, patient being, filled with energy – not a mean, controlling, hateful, judgmental God. I've come to know and sense a source of great love from God, my higher power, and that has helped me to heal more than anything because I frequently asked this God for help and it came. There are times, with certain people, the word "God" brings up images and feelings of dread. The God I know now is the one that frequently calls me to more challenging places in my heart and soul and life. I know when some of you hear the word "God" it brings up negative feelings and the word can be scary. I get that. I understand. You can call what your "knowing" tells you anything you want, and if the word "God" brings up bad feelings, find your own word for it. The word God was a problem for me, too. I would feel this instant, "I am a sinning piece of crap," and God is "The great rule enforcer." I'm ok with that word today. There's been enough time for me to make peace with that childhood idea of God. I was raised in a conservative religion, so doing good deeds, following rules, and praying certain salvation prayers was pretty normal. I knew I no longer wanted to do good things out of fear of retribution or Hell. I wanted to do them because of love, because I felt it inside and wanted to share or help another. My inner spirituality went from FEAR to LOVE.

The God I've come to know deep in my soul is full of lovingkindness; patient, generous, compassionate, inclusive, and loves every human, yes, even those that the church deems sinful or unworthy of God. God's love has no boundaries, it pours out like a waterfall on every human. No matter what we've ever done or are doing, all human beings are unconditionally loved and accepted.

I have more questions and less answers about who God is all the time and I'm okay with that. When I was a kid, all the churches seemed to have to have their "answers." I remember having pause though, when they gave me their *answers*…it wouldn't set well with me. Inside, I disagreed and eventually I realized that no one has all the answers. No one. And, if someone tells me they have the absolute answers, I smile and move on because I follow "the knowing." I am no longer in fear, but in love.

I've had to work and seek, very passionately, for many years, to believe that God is not angry with me; that God does not hate me; that God is not to blame for my abuse. I am not to blame for my abuse. God did not cause my abuse so good would come out of it. I was taught that God is in control of everything, all the time, which made me feel like, "What the hell? If you are in control, God, then you could have stopped my abusers? Instead, You looked on as I was sexually assaulted? Screw you!!!"

That wasn't true, the God I know abhors any type of abuse. And as far as *control*, I believe that we have free will. "God's control" doesn't have to be definitively answered for me… that's for the theologians to argue over. I believe God gave over control when he made humans free to love and hate. These are just my beliefs, and you may disagree. That's okay! I'm not a Bible Scholar or claim to have answers to the big questions (and IMHO no one has all the answers)—however, I do know what my heart feels, and listen to the spirit inside me. The knowing is there and it's my journey.

I believe my parents did the best they knew how when raising me and I respect and love them for that. My mom tells a story of our family car being "some kind of stick shift." She didn't know how to drive this particular car, but nonetheless, she put me in that car as a baby and prayed the traffic lights would cooperate so she didn't have to stop while driving me to church, LOL. She was dedicated! She believed this was what I needed to get the best start in life, and she decided to be brave and drive that car and me to church every Sunday. I love her for that.

I loved all of my Sunday school teachers; and I believe that they and the pastors and all of those people in my childhood religion had good, loving intentions toward me. They were genuinely fearful of God's wrath and Hell, and they were kind enough to warn me. I'm grateful I was raised in the church. I learned so much and it caused so many questions for me. In fact, if I hadn't had such an upbringing, I may not have searched so hard and long for the loving God I know now. For that, for them, I am truly, forever grateful. The church also caused me unnecessary, great pain and shame over the years.

My own understanding, after spending many hours alone and many years with the God that I sense inside me and out there and everywhere, is that every person on the planet has been given free will and choice. My abusers and your abusers had free choice to abuse and our abusers also had their own pain, mental illness, hurt, and were probably abused themselves. Please DO NOT hear me excusing abuse here, because I'm not. I once heard and agree with the fact that, "There are always 'reasons' for bad behavior, but never 'excuses.'"

I've come to realize that being honest and deeply authentic with myself, others and God/Universe is the road to freedom. It sets me free and gives me the peace that surpasses all understanding. God loves me so deeply that as I am my authentic self, people will either love me or not. I am okay with that!

For many years, I had a stream of bitterness flowing through me that I would slam down, as if I was playing that old game,

Whack-A-Mole. I felt bitter anger inside and had flashbacks about the words of criticism, the beatings, and the teen sexual assaults that I'd endured. I would be happy and enjoying my day and, just as a sun-darkening black storm cloud sneaks up on a sun-kissed day, a feeling of anger would stream through my veins. I'd feel bitter. I'd spew negativity throughout my mind and, at times, on anyone in my path.

For example, one day on a vacation at the beach, before my therapy work, I was reading a book and I paused a moment, staring out into space as a memory of an abuse emerged. Simultaneously, my young son innocently asked for some cheese crackers. I snapped back at him, "We just finished lunch!" I remember the look on his little face of joy as it turned to fear and confusion. I quickly apologized, of course, but the damage had been done. Ugh. I felt awful. There was that familiar feeling of shame. Can you relate? That precious boy asking for cheese crackers didn't make me angry. Anger was already streaming through from someplace else completely. That's how our unhealed shame and anger is dumped onto others. That's why it must be uncovered, felt and processed with a safe person or therapist. A seven-year-old doesn't understand shame. My son just knew his mommy's face was angry and disapproving of him (which wasn't even about him). That scenario could have been any of my children.

I wish with everything I am that I could take those times back but, of course, I can't. What I can do, and have done at times, is take responsibility, apologize, and live in gratefulness that the bitter stream seems to have been turned into a sweet river of compassion, grace and acceptance. The stream no longer runs bitter; it runs with a sweet, loving-kindness and a knowing that *hurt people*, well, they *hurt people*. I had unhealed hurt inside me and, therefore, I was hurting the people that I love.

The shame of abuse made me feel that I needed other people's approval to be okay. I was codependent on other's thoughts about me. I allowed other people's opinions of me to influence *my* opinion of me. If others thought I was okay, I followed their lead and thought I was okay. If people thought I was not okay, I would spiral into shame, beat myself up and hide even harder. Can you relate? It's painful. It's lonely. It's certainly frustrating.

At times, I felt I didn't want to go on here on earth. I had allowed other people to have power over me and to influence how I felt about me. At some point, through all I was doing to heal, I decided to be there for myself and to stop judging myself and hating myself. I chose to love me and have compassion on that little girl inside me who had endured shame, criticism, beatings and abuse, and also on that young, teenaged girl that was sexually assaulted. She needed me to stand by her and love her and we needed self-compassion.

I love Rachel Platten's song, *Fight Song,* and I listened to it frequently:

> *Like a small boat*
> *On the ocean*
> *Sending big waves*
> *Into motion*
> *Like how a single word*
> *Can make a heart open*
> *I might only have one match*
> *But I can make an explosion*

And all those things I didn't say
Wrecking balls inside my brain
I will scream them loud tonight
Can you hear my voice this time?
This is my fight song
Take back my life song
Prove I'm alright song
My power's turned on
Starting right now
I'll be strong
I'll play my fight song
And I don't really care if nobody else believes '
Cause I've still got a lot of fight left in me.

I also resonate on a deep level with Kesha's song, *Praying,* as she sings to her abuser:

Oh, but after everything you've done
I can thank you for how strong I have become
'Cause you brought the flames and you put me through hell
I had to learn how to fight for myself
And we both know all the truth
I could tell I'll just say this is "I wish you farewell"
I hope you're somewhere prayin', prayin'
I hope your soul is changin', changin'
I hope you find your peace
Falling on your knees, prayin'
I'm proud of who I am
No more monsters, I can breathe again
And you said that I was done
Well, you were wrong and now the best is yet to come.

I began to look for love and goodness, and I, too, desired to be a loving force in the world for others. Like ocean waves, love seemed to lap onto me and melt my heart more because I was asking for it. I don't know much about the Law of Attraction, neither have I read any of books on the subject. However, experientially, I know there's something to it as far as love and bitterness are concerned.

I know that, whenever I sought justification for my anger, it seemed to multiply! And I could find plenty of other people in my pain field to be angry along with me. I found being angry and talking about my pain from abuse all the time attracted other people in pain. It also attracted more anger into my life. There's a small payoff, for sure, because I could remain a victim. I'd been wronged! Friends were sad for me, pitied me. They were even angry for me. But I got sick and tired of being angry and talking about myself. I got tired of feeling bitter and powerless.

There is a much greater payoff that I discovered when I came to the end of my anger. When I sought healing and forgiveness, that, too, came my way. I wanted to become a person I admired. For me, that meant I needed to mature and grow. One thing I've learned is that no matter what your age, you don't mature and grow automatically; YOU HAVE TO WANT IT! There are 80-year-old people who are bitter and angry and have never matured or grown up.

The good news is that no matter what your age, you always have an opportunity to grow and evolve. I knew I had to stop starting, and being a part of, gossip and drama. I had to be alone if that's what it took. I had to evaluate my friendships. I asked myself, "Do they talk about people? Are they focused on the negative and do they bring me down?" I had to have some hard talks with friends, and I had to let some friends go. I realized there were people that would build into me and encourage me in my life. I learned to spend more time with them and to cherish them. They are very special. It's true that we attract what we are in at any given time. I had to become someone whom I admired and desired to become in order to have those types of friends. I've not perfected this, but it's not a normal part of me anymore.

Over some years, more friends that were seeking love, healing and forgiveness showed up in my life. I didn't even know healing was possible. I didn't believe it could be real for me. I knew I didn't want a fake healing. I wanted permanent, for real, healing. I wanted to be healed of this gnawing pain; to be free of its grip on my life.

Healing is a little different for everyone. For me, it was not magic. For me, healing was not easy. Healing didn't come in an instant flash of light. Other people I've talked to have had different experiences from my own. Many women have had anything but an easy childhood. Yet, when some are asked how they've healed and forgiven their perpetrators, they reply, "God healed me. I can't explain how, but God just healed me and I know I'm healed and I hold no ill feelings toward them." I wish I could have had that kind of healing. I definitely did not. I tried to push it way down and thought I forgave and even tried to believe it. But for me, it kept coming up and out and spilling all over my life like bleach on red carpet.

I remember thinking maybe something's wrong with me. I'd been working my therapy for a few years, meditating, journaling, and seeking. My process was a slow, brutal process. My process was full of therapy work and journaling. All I wanted to do was run away! I had to work hard for my freedom and healing. For me, it took great persistence. My healing paths came through therapy, energy work, yoga, books, prayer, vulnerability, humility and feeling the pain. I wish I could tell you that I asked the God of my under-standing for healing, and *voilà,* I was miraculously healed. That may happen for you. Everyone's journeys are different. Healing, for me, was day after day, week after week, painstakingly *putting into action* what I learned in therapy, reading good, recommended books, and listening to that small quiet voice inside every day.

I had to notice my self-loathing, shaming self-talk and write it down. I had to change my self-talk with a re-parenting voice of loving-kindness and patience, every day after day after day after day. Over 35+ years that protective, bossy voice tried to get me in line, and I finally had to put a stop to it. Not only did I have to put a stop to it, I had to reform it and believe in myself for the first time. It's been my personal experience, that I had to go *through* my problem areas, my pain, my hurt, and I just couldn't go *around* or *over* or *under* them. I had to go *through* them. I had to learn to feel them and try hard to stand firm not to escape them.

I've experienced many setbacks on the road to healing and also many high points. One great turning point for me was attending The Haven Retreat in Utah. This is an amazing place to heal from any kind of sexual abuse. They have counselors that lead groups, counselors that educate on the process of healing, yoga, Tai Chi, and many other activities that are helpful and healing. Another great part of my experience is that I was with 30 other women, sexual abuse survivors, ranging in age from 20-68 years old. It's never too late to heal your past. Never. I'm so grateful I was able to go. Each morning, I would get up before any of the other women, grab a cup of coffee and a blanket and head out to the back deck in the cold morning air. I was sitting at the base of some of the most beautiful, glorious mountains I'd ever seen. It was awe-inspiring. One morning, with my journal and pen in hand, I was seeking genuinely for answers and guidance. With all my heart, I wanted real change, real release from the vengefulness and bitterness. In my knowing, I sensed, and heard:

> "How much longer are you willing to give your power away to your abusers? Haven't they occupied enough of your life? Haven't they taken enough? Don't you want to let go of the vengeance and take back the power that rightly belongs to you and let it take you to great places you've never been before? Don't you want to take back that power and let it help you and use it for helping others? You can have your power back. This is up to you, Cindy. You can release all of this. You can be free. You truly hold all the power, but when you hold onto the past, you're actually handing your power over to another. It's your choice!"

At that moment, I remember saying out loud with conviction, "Yes, I agree. Enough is enough. I choose take my power back now!"

Taking my power back was more freeing than I could imagine, and I felt lighter than I'd felt in years. I felt a peace and joy for the first time in a long time. Part of taking my power back involved letting go of being a victim, not allowing the memories or the vengeance toward those that hurt me, stomp their big loud feet through my thought life any longer. I was ready to choose to walk right over to that bitterness and to those who hurt me and *take*, not ask, for my personal power back. I was no longer going to wallow in my hurt and anger. I was taking charge of my heart and life and deciding that I mattered enough to fight for freedom from these debilitating feelings. I was going to have compassion for those abusers knowing, they too, had been abused or hurt to be able to do what they did. Deciding to take charge of my life would allow me to do all the amazing things I'd dreamed of and have fun doing them! I did just that on that morning, on that porch, before an audience of those magnificent, giant, regal mountains. Streams of thoughts came through me over the next few days. One such stream was that the people who hurt me did so because they, too, were very much in pain and were hurting.

As these streams of "knowings" came up inside me - I would feel it so deeply - tears of compassion would run down my face. I didn't excuse my abusers' behaviors at all. People need to be held accountable and suffer the consequences for their actions.

I was no longer going to allow my life to be poisoned with bitterness. I was done. I was no longer going to wait for or expect anything from my abusers: not apologies, and not remorse. That would be nice, but to expect anything from them would be handing over to them, the power of my healing. That's not power, that's helplessness. I wasn't interested in that.

I wanted to hold all the power to heal. "My pain may not be my fault, but it is my responsibility to heal." One day, I saw a meme on Facebook with that very statement. Some of the comments below the meme were really angry, commenting that the statement means that the victim had some responsibility. That's not what it means to me. We have no choice when it comes to being abused by someone older or stronger than us. We are not responsible, and no abuse is *ever* the victim's fault. We may be victims as children, but we don't have to stay victims. Instead, it's our privilege and empowerment when we take personal responsibility to do what we need to do to take care of ourselves and our mental/emotional health. That's self-love. We get to heal and grow and feel good and take our power back! I remember thinking the people who did those things to me should have to pay for my therapy, they should have to be responsible for my healing. That's possible in some cases, I guess, but not likely. Something inside me always wants justice, but that's just not going to happen here on earth all the time. I wasn't going to let anything hold me back! I refused to have my life held hostage by someone else, waiting to see whether or not they would take responsibility.

The power to heal was mine, and I knew it deep in my heart. Your power to get better and feel good, is yours! You can do it. If I can overcome my angst and heal, I believe anyone can.

It was time for me to choose to walk away, to wish my offenders their own healing, and to get on with all I was destined to do on this wonderful planet for the years I'm here. I was walking away from all the resentment - for good! I knew I would be a fool to allow this to ruin any more days, months or years of my life. Staying in pain and waiting for my offenders to take responsibility for my healing, would be giving my power away. I need my power to live, and to love, and to be someone who I could admire! This was anunforgettable experience for me. That day, at the foot of the mountains, was one of those "ah-ha" moments. I'll carry this experience and day, and Haven Retreat in my heart forever.

I've learned not to judge my own healing path or anyone else's healing path. I've learned not to compare my life or my healing to anyone else's life or healing. It truly is fruitless. I'm not going to say, "Well, God must love that woman more because she was healed instantly." That wouldn't be the truth. We all heal differently. I had to go to therapy and work on knowing myself better. I had to become a student of me. Therapy was life-changing for me. In fact, I would pay double, even triple the time and money to heal *because it feels so good on this side of it.*

One of the reasons I wanted to write this book is to have a compilation of healing things that all of us who've experienced various abuses can use. I learn so much from hearing someone else's authentic journey. That's why I want to share my authentic story and those of some clients who also wanted to share. I haven't "arrived." I don't believe anyone "arrives." But we grow and we heal. I love healed, peaceful headspace. It's so much better than insecure, angry, fake headspace.

My clients tell me that when I tell them my personal recovery stories, it helps them the most. I think that is because I'm not just teaching them how to heal. I'm telling them I've been there, I've been through it, and I've come to a place of joy, confidence and emotional freedom. Writing or speaking is the best way I can think of to convey the message that healing IS possible, and that I experienced a genuine change of heart, from bitter, angry, pain-filled victim to joy-filled and grateful, possessing genuine happiness that allows me to do what I love to do every day. I believe it's possible for you, too! You will have your own demons or feelings from which you will want to be free. They may not necessarily be like mine, and that's okay. We're all unique people with our own feelings, and they all matter!

The best news ever to a person who has experienced painful abuse and has spent years in bitterness, hurt and debilitating rage and anger or quiet misery in isolation, is there truly is hope for change! We can be free!

I want to share a part of a story from *The Velveteen Rabbit,* by Marjorie Williams. It's been very meaningful to me over the years. It is the story of a stuffed rabbit that yearns to become real through the genuine love of its owner.

"The Skin Horse had lived longer in the nursery than any of the others. He was so old that his brown coat was bald in patches and showed the seams underneath, and most of the hairs in his tail had been pulled out to string bead necklaces. He was wise, for he had seen a long succession of mechanical toys arrive to boast and swagger, and by-and-by break their mainsprings and pass away, and he knew that they were only toys, and would never turn into anything else. For nursery magic is very strange and wonderful, and only those playthings that are old and wise and experienced like the Skin Horse understand all about it.

"What is REAL?" asked the Rabbit one day, when they were lying side by side near the nursery fender, before Nana came to tidy the room. "Does it mean having things that buzz inside you and a stick-out handle?"

"Real isn't how you are made," said the Skin Horse. "It's a thing that happens to you. When a child loves you for a long, long time, not just to play with, but REALLY loves you, then you become Real."

"Does it hurt?" asked the Rabbit.

"Sometimes," said the Skin Horse, for he was always truthful. "When you are Real you don't mind being hurt."

"Does it happen all at once, like being wound up," he asked, "or bit by bit?"

"It doesn't happen all at once," said the Skin Horse. "You become. It takes a long time. That's why it doesn't happen often to people who break easily, or have sharp edges, or who have to be carefully kept. Generally, by the time you are Real, most of your hair has been loved off, and your eyes drop out and you get loose in the joints and very shabby. But these things don't matter at all, because once you are Real you can't be ugly, except to people who don't understand."

"I suppose *you* are real?" said the Rabbit. And then he wished he had not said it, for he thought the Skin Horse might be sensitive. But the Skin Horse only smiled.

"The Boy's Uncle made me Real," he said. "That was a great many years ago; but once you are Real you can't become unreal again. It lasts for always."

We can love ourselves into realness too! We can become the CEO's of our own lives and wellness. We have the power to help ourselves. We have what it takes to love ourselves genuinely. In fact, we have to love ourselves to truly feel loved…depending on others for that self-love is impossible - and it turns into codependence. It's every man and woman's responsibility to find out how to love themselves. To make a way to truly love and care for themselves. Anything else is dependence. And, it's okay and amazing to be loved by others! I'm not saying go to an island alone. I'm saying that deep, inside job of self-love, is ours alone to do! No one can do this for us. We can't fake this. We can't phone this in!

Once I began to truly love me, I began to become real and authentic. For me, if everyone left me, decided not to love me, walked away and/or blamed me, I would be sad no doubt. But would I be alone, and want to die? No! I would love myself and find new people! I think some times that human fear around being alone with no one and possibly not surviving, keeps many people staying in the same toxic circles of people. I did that for many years, and I was literally dying inside because my knowings were telling me to grow and learn and move, and I was staying in the same cycles of toxicity, thinking I was safe. I may have been physically safe, but I was not mentally or spiritually safe in those circles. I had to break out and see if there were good, evolving people out there. I have found that there are amazing, loving, genuine people every-where I go! My love for myself grew in the "garden" of growing people and therapy. It made me feel safe enough to finally be real, authentic, and exactly who I *am*. No longer would I allow others to define me. No longer would I allow other's love, hate or criticism for me affect my love for me. I practiced love for myself every day by speaking to myself with self-compassion and self-kindness. I've referred to this before, but Jesus said, "Love others as (just like) you love yourself." And as I practice that love day by day, I am able to be real and take my power back and continue to heal my life. I want to make it clear that I have to practice this *every day*. Almost every day I journal and I seek answers. It seems to come easier for me as the years go on.

Friend, you have what it takes. If someone as messed up as I was, can heal and change and become someone I admire today, I promise you can, too! Anything is possible. I believe that with all my heart. You deserve to be *your own* support even if no one else supports you. Never stop asking for what you need. Ask again and again. Never give up on you. Believe in yourself. If you stop believ-ing, ASK the higher power of your understanding for more faith to believe in your worth!

JOURNAL PROMPTS

- Which things, from the above list, do you use to numb your feelings?
- Have you ever felt like staying in bed and/or checking out of your life?
- Can you identify anger or resentment that may need your attention?
- How would your life be different if you went on a healing journey and could be your authentic self, if you could use your unique gifts in the world?
- What do you believe about God? Do you even know? Do you want to know?
- How would it feel to be empowered, to take your power back from your abusers, and to stop feeling like a victim?
- What do you want or need to ASK for?

Chapter 3

Let Go of People-Pleasing and Set Boundaries

"Ciiindyyyy!" My friend seemed to drag my name out forever. "You need to find your voice!" My friend was frustrated. "Say what you need to say! Stop letting these people get away with this!" I would be asked to do something, want to say "no," but instead, freeze and say "yes." I was unable to say "no." My friend was clearly concerned for me. As a young adult, I allowed certain people to control me. When we have abuse in our past, as children, often we take on this victim, mousey mentality. We apologize non-stop... we are annoying. We allow people to continue to manipulate, control, and abuse us. My friend said again, "Take responsibility for your own life!" Ugh, those were such tough words to hear.

Flannery O'Connor said, "The truth does not change according to our ability to stomach it."

Is that ever the truth my stomach was feeling! My friend was tired of me not standing up for myself, not having my own back, taking what was dished out, and then whining about it. She was a trooper for hanging in there with me. Why she did, I don't know, but I so appreciate friends who tell me the truth.

I felt helpless, hopeless, and powerless to stand up and speak my mind to anyone, except for my husband of course, LOL. When I thought about speaking my mind, I would cringe inside. I would find myself wanting to stay in my house and close all the blinds. I felt like a mute mouse. Remember Gus in the Disney cartoon movie, *Cinderella*? I loved Gus. He couldn't speak for himself either because of his intense fear of the wicked stepmother and the cat, Lucifer. Cinderella's love for Gus, all her kindness and nurturing, brought him out of his shell. He, then, was able to become a very happy-go-lucky little mouse, speaking his mind. Standing tall and walking confidently, Gus finally was able to even speak his mind to the clever, bullying cat, Lucifer.

I would prepare to say "no" to the next person that asked me to help with whatever, and then, I would cave in and say "yes." I couldn't see my way out. I felt like I was trying to punch my way out of a wet brown paper bag. I felt angry and resentful. I mistakenly thought, "*These people* need to change, not me! Why do I have to change? They should change! They need to stop asking me for things! They need to take care of their own responsibilities!" When I came to the end of my rant, and my tears, I realized *these people* didn't have to do anything. *I* was the one who needed to change. Me. I can only control me. No one else. My friend is a good friend, the very best. If you have a friend that will tell you the truth no matter how much it stings, you have a gem of infinite worth.

I can almost pinpoint where my boundary-less-ness began. As a little girl, I felt powerless. Being powerless made me feel like I was nothing, unimportant, even insignificant. Kids sometimes feel like they should stay out of the way, be small and be quiet. They feel they don't deserve to give their opinion about anything. When kids speak up, many times, they're shot down.

"You don't know what you're talking about!"

"If you don't have something nice to say, shut your mouth!" It's actually dangerous for a child to not have their voice. Children without voices are prime targets for abusers. Abusers seek out the children with low self-esteem, no voice, no power.

I believe one common parenting style can perpetuate this voice-less, powerlessness in children. This is not a parenting book, but stay with me here. The *Authoritarian Parenting Style* tends to be controlling and has high expectations with little feedback and little to no nurturing. Feedback, when given, is mostly criticism which leads to shame. Mistakes are punished harshly. Yelling and corporal punishment are common. The resulting effect on children raised with Authoritarian Style is the false self-belief that, "If I'm not obedient, I'm not loved." It also produces fearfulness; low self-esteem; a tendency to conform easily; anxiety and depression. They struggle with self-control because they aren't given choices to experience natural consequences. This has been a very popular parenting style for many decades. Kid's should be seen and not heard! These were the broken tools passed down generation after generation even into my own children's generation…until, I began to read modern-day parenting books, about parenting by grace instead of corporal punishment. I'm so grateful that my generation, when I was raising my kids, began to have a plethora of books published on parenting through positive reinforcement, choices, grace, and loving discipline. I know my parents didn't have access to these types of resources.

"Young ladies, you are all going to the principal's office!" I was a mischievous child. Yes, that was me splashing the water fountain water all over the locker room floor with my little friends while we laughed and skated in the water joyously and uproariously until the always very serious, mustached, deep-voiced, gym teacher would hear the ruckus behind the locker room door. He'd fling it open in time to witness five to six out of control 9-year-olds having a field day. He blew his loud whistle, grimaced and demanded we come out to the gym, immediately. I was always an instigator of mischief (and laughter), especially with my peers. I have always loved seeing people laugh and laughing myself… Boy, did that trait ever get me into trouble! It also got me a semi-annual "N" (*Needs Improvement*) in self-control on my grade school report cards. (Just the other day, my parents gave me a box filled with pictures, art and report cards from my childhood. Almost every report card had at least one "N" in self-control! LOL)

I think as young as four years old, I began to notice that the adults around me had two speeds that could change on a dime: smiles with approval or angry faces. The adults were happy when I obeyed and angry and loud when I didn't. My 4-year-old brain learned to scan adults regularly to see which face they were wearing (happy or angry). I was always assessing. Today, I just want to hug that little 4-year-old girl and say, "Honey, it's all going to be okay. Adults are serious but life really doesn't have to be. You're fine, girlfriend!"

My client, Kendall's, story:
As a little girl, I loved playing in my room alone. As long as my mom was busy and not nagging me to get outside with the other kids, I could play for hours. I often got away with being in my bedroom for a great deal of time. I would use my closet door as a chalkboard and I would teach my dolls and animals everything I'd learned at school that week. Sometimes, I would hide inside my closet (I have never been a fan of noise and my house was loud).

I'd push the clothes back and set up a flashlight on the side shelf and pretend it was my secret office. I would write in my cherished blue, three-ring binder, full of luscious notebook paper. I absolutely loved paper, pens, and writing. You can go anywhere in a story. I remember I wanted so badly to be Harriet, from *Harriet the Spy* - a book by Louise Fitzhugh, that my 4th grade teacher, Mrs. Schmidt, read to our class on sunny afternoons while we sat in a circle on the cold, tile floor of our classroom. Being read to by my teacher was one of my very favorite activities in elementary school. She had a soothing voice that made me feel safe. I felt important, knowing that she would spend time with me, even if it was in a group. Just like Harriet, I would hide in the bushes with my binder and write down every juicy tidbit of conversation. My heart always beat a little faster when I saw pens, pencils, notebook paper, chalk and markers. Those items were my some of my most valued possessions. It may seem strange for a child to want to be alone instead of running outside with the neighborhood kids, but early on, I was an introvert. I loved working independently. I loved writing and creating. I loved everything to do with learning and teaching.

Some days, a cloud of darkness would come over my bedroom as I heard my mother, in another part of the house, begin to scream and pound her feet on the floor as she came closer. Was she coming for me? I would ascend into a heightened state of alert, especially if mom was angry. My little brain knew that it was not going to end well. My mom was unpredictable. Minor messes could quickly send her into an all-out fury. Her home was kept perfectly. If things were "out of order," as she frequently said, she would instantly begin looking for the guilty party. She would begin yelling and swinging the belt or the wooden spoon. She would become enraged when she was mad, and she would come find me if she thought I needed to be punished. She would grit her teeth and her eyes would bulge out like Large Marge in *Pee Wee Herman's Big Adventure*. I remember being frozen and terrified of her unbridled anger and her scan of the house searching for someone to blame.

I remember one day, walking up to my house from the school bus with my little sister. We both knew we had to be on alert those first moments coming in from school. We never talked about it, but we looked at each other at times walking down our front walk and we both knew what each other was thinking. We would either smell the clean scent of Pine Sol along with the aroma of spaghetti and meatballs wafting out from the screen door (this meant Mom was in a good mood and our re-entry to the house would probably be seamless) or we would smell nothing. On this particular day she was waiting for us behind the screen door, hands on her hips, brows furrowed. My stomach dropped as we walked in. She grabbed us both by our hair. We would brace ourselves inside for the storm that was about to hit. She began screaming, slapping us, and pounding us with her fists. She led my little sister and me down the hallway to our shared bedroom where, earlier that day, she had pulled out and flung every drawer from our dressers, onto the floor. There were drawers sideways, upside down, completely askew. Every piece of our underwear, socks and clothing was scattered onto the floor or up onto the curtain rods. She even pulled the mattresses and rose-flowered sheets off of our twin beds and flung them. It was as if a tornado had come through our bedroom. She threw both of us into our room by our hair and slammed the door, screaming, "Don't come out until it's clean!" SLAM! My sister and I stood there for a minute, facing each other. Eventually, our eyes met. We pursed our lips, our eyes welled up with tears, and we began sobbing while we held hands and looked around our bedroom. We felt scared and helpless. We were overwhelmed. We didn't know where to begin. We couldn't lift our mattresses. We were little girls, and we couldn't possibly reach the clothing on the curtain rods. At the same time, we both knew mom meant what she said. We had to figure it out, and so we began.

After some hours of working together to get the drawers back in, I began to wonder when Dad would be home. Was he coming home tonight? Would he be out of town? Would we be alone with her, and her rage, all night? When I was a little girl, I noticed mom never 'lost it' when dad was home. And she could be brutally out of control when he wasn't. When Dad was around, she would only give us mean looks or speak sharply to us in a whisper. We were so afraid of mom, her anger and the beatings, that when she would reach across the dinner table to grab the ketchup, we all ducked and put our hands in front of our faces. It was nothing for her to slap us right across our faces. These were the years where shame was put inside me, inside my heart. I remember feeling like a terrible being, a pain in the ass, always a burden. I began feeling sure I was bad on the inside, like I couldn't help myself. I began to realize that there were no boundaries around her physical strength and no level of respect for our cries of pain. I think these years were when I began to become a people-pleaser. I thought, "If I could please mom, she would be civil, she may even laugh, especially if I imitated my grade school teachers." I remember often seeing her grimaced face and asking, "Are you okay, Mom?"

End of Kendall's Story

I believe that children who are taught to people please are more vulnerable to all types of abuse. A pattern of trying to be perfect, of staying out of trouble so as not to disappoint their parents, leaves children with the idea that if they make their parents (people) happy, "they will love me." They learn to be excellent people pleasers, door mats, and targets for abusers.

What does parenting have to do with becoming a boundaryless, people-pleaser? Everything! Earlier, I referenced the authoritarian parenting style because it makes clear the "why" and the "how" of children becoming boundaryless people-pleasers. This is important for two reasons: 1) without boundaries, we can more easily become the victims of abuse; and 2) people-pleasing teaches us that what other people think and want is more important than what we think and want. It causes us to doubt ourselves and to doubt our gut feelings, and throws us into codependency.

The authoritarian parenting style says, "I am the parent! I am in charge!" It emphasizes obedience. This is a dictatorship! The child isn't given choices. Basically, it says, "Do what I say or else!" I think a lot of well-meaning parents, including myself with my children, regrettably, were trying to get through the daily pressures of life, and saw that this style of parenting works to get their children to obey. Most parents do not set out or intend to be bad parents; however, this much too common parenting style fosters broken relationships between parent and child. It creates a "you against me" dynamic. The child's feelings can be summed up as: "I'll be loved and smiled at if I'm good, and I'll be a disappointment, punished and maybe outcast from the family circle if I'm bad." Sounds somewhat like some religions, right? Did you feel like that when you were a child?

I'm convinced this is where children get the idea that adults have the right to cross children's boundaries. I learned that adults had the final say and if I did what the adults wanted, everything was okay. My mom told me as I started school, "If you get a swat at school, you're going to get it ten times worse at home!" I learned, as a child, that the adults carried all the power. This style of parenting, while it may get immediate results, creates an unhealthy obedience and a lack of critical thinking.

Today, I like to watch my son, Matt, parent. He has a two-year-old son name Christopher, who is probably the most adorable 2-year-old ever born. Of course, he is my grandson! He behaves like a typical 2-year-old. Every once in a while, Christopher will walk around the family room and wail one of his little dinosaurs toward someone. Matt and my daughter-in-law, Carly, will tell him in a soft tone to be gentle and not to throw his toys at people. Predictably, he'll end up doing the same thing again five minutes later. Matt comes along and puts his arms around Christopher and gently says, "Christopher, we don't throw toys at people because it could hurt them. I know you don't want to hurt Pawpaw, so don't throw your dinosaur at him." If Christopher still doesn't get the message, Matt will explain why he's putting Christopher, or the dinosaur, in time-out. Christopher smiles and begins playing happily again until the next time he tests his daddy's love. Then Matt does the same loving exercise with him. No matter what the behavior is, Christopher continues to be in the circle of love with his parents. This is called *Authoritative Parenting Style*. It blends a caring tone with structure and consistent limit setting. This fosters a healthy, open, caring relationship between parent and child.

Christopher is turning three in a couple of weeks and I commented to Carly recently, "He has this happy, kind, gentle way about him." Christopher is learning that, no matter what he does, there may be consequences, but he will be hugged, loved and talked to gently. This tells him, most importantly, that he matters and he's loved - that he is enough.

Children without boundaries or without the right to say "no" or without the ability to make some choices, end up being at the mercy of adults who may try to hurt them or abuse them. They've learned they have no power and that the adult has all the power. I learned early on that my "no" or my boundaries, had zero clout with adults.

My own addiction to people-pleasing spiraled out of control. It was all about me. It was deeper than helping someone out, being a kind person, making someone else happy, giving someone what they wanted. Oh, all the sneaky ways I referred to it! It was much deeper. I was trying to get something I desperately needed by doing all these things - value. I needed value… value to someone, anyone. The question, "Am I valuable?" begins very early in life when parents who don't value themselves don't have the tools to give value to their children, no matter how well-meaning the parents are. The lack of knowing your value and being able to mirror that value to your child travels through generation after generation.

The unhealed generational pattern was like poison running through my ancestors' blood. It had been flowing through my bloodline for decades. It flowed like this:

"If I take care of the people who are sick or broken, they may have the resources to love me."

This unhealed pattern was now a part of me and a part of my generation. I didn't have a clue how to change it for my children.

Eventually, I decided this pattern required some personal exploration.

"Am I worthy?" I would ask myself. The answer kept coming back, "No, you are not worthy. You are not valuable, you are not enough, unless you do this, or have that house, or this amount of money, or drive that car, or look like this or look like that." Therefore, many of us began making attempts to fix it. Now it was my turn to look at the mountain of evidence of "not worthy enough" in my own heart.

Am I valuable? Do I matter? Am I worthy? Am I enough? "No," was the default answer. I wanted to answer, "Yes." So I began to do whatever was necessary to achieve, "Yes, I am valuable. I matter. I'm worthy. I'm enough."

Many of us try different avenues to achieve, "Yes, you are worthy" status such as outward beauty, intelligence, sex, decorating, efficiency, responsibility and perfection. Not one of those things delivered a steadfast "yes" to those nagging questions of value and worth for me. No matter how much I went the extra mile for someone else, or took responsibility for someone else's mess, or bent over backwards to bail someone out of their problems, I was NOT enough in my own heart. I would lay down my own life to help 'fix' someone else's life. This is codependency.

No matter how hard I tried, how hard I worked, the "Yes, you are enough," never stuck for very long. It came occasionally, but it lasted only a short time, sometimes an hour, sometimes a day, sometimes a week, but before long, some force inside wanted me to prove that I deserved a "Yes, you are enough," again.

On and on it continued, until I was exhausted, depressed, anxious, and frozen on my couch under a blanket. I couldn't keep up with my heart's demand to hear a "yes" from anybody to the question, "Am I valuable?" I couldn't keep up with the requests from others because once people realize that you will drop everything and come to their rescue, they come to you from out of the woodwork. You can't really blame them. Who wouldn't want to rely on someone else to help take care of their responsibilities.

I was like a heroin addict. I needed another fix, more, and then, more after that. The need was insatiable. Am I enough? Am I enough? Am I enough? I would say "yes" to all requests. I would help whomever I could, and I thought, "They will give me a 'yes,' however temporary." I needed a fix for my self-esteem, NOW! I would do whatever it took to get my need met, until I hit rock bottom. I couldn't answer calls anymore. I couldn't get off my couch. I couldn't do one more thing. During my teen years, I was even more boundaryless and people-pleasing. I talk to so many young girls in my practice and I hear that their first sexual encounter was like, "It just happened. It slipped in. Before I knew it, he was inside." That was many of my friends' experiences, too. How about you? Do you remember your first time? Was it planned or did it just happen? When parenting styles foster *obedience* over *choices* many girls grow up to be teens who find themselves without the power to firmly say "no."

Once I became an adult, I was a card-carrying member of the boundaryless, people-pleaser committee. I found myself wanting to avoid the church, the PTA, and some friends because I would be asked to lead this, help with that, teach these children, bring food here at this time, head up the summer vacation camp, start this committee. My "No, I will not be able to do that," button was broken. I ended up saying "yes" every time I really meant "no." I became resentful and then I began to avoid people.

Have you ever felt like you just wanted to be left alone because you already had enough on your to-do list? I didn't have boundaries. I was inauthentic. I couldn't deny any request because of my fear of what people would think of me and I desperately wanted them to like me. What if they thought I was lazy? What if they thought I wasn't a team player? What if they thought I didn't care? What if they talked about me behind my back because I wasn't willing to help? What if they didn't like me? I was so wrapped up in how others thought and felt about me that what I thought or felt didn't matter.

I blamed other people because I couldn't say "no." I remember being angry with people, gossiping about how bossy or pushy they were. Until I realized, "this" was on me. I had never learned boundaries for myself. I didn't know it was possible to say "no" and smile and not cause the sky to fall, or that saying "no" wouldn't cause me to lose connections with people.

Then there was an awakening for me, a time when I'd had it with all my responsibilities. I couldn't do or commit to one more thing and I had some type of breakdown. This constant stress and strain eventually caused illness in my body. I found myself on my couch, exhausted, impatient with my kids, depressed, eating carbs like it was nobody's business, and basically, doing nothing. I ended up in the hospital with stomach pain so bad that I couldn't eat without severe pain. While at the hospital, a bunch of tests were run on me with no answers. They couldn't find anything wrong with me. One nurse cleared my mom and Steve out of my room and asked, "Are you afraid of your husband?" They assumed since I was sick with no answers maybe I was being abused and afraid to tell anyone, so I became ill. This is a real thing with faux symptoms in the body! My sick stomach issues were psychosomatic. My mind had made my body sick. I had genuine symptoms but nothing could be found to contribute to them. My therapist wisely said, "Cindy, you have to learn to set boundaries or you may end up with a serious illness." She gave me a book called, *Boundaries: How to Say Yes, How to Say No and Take Control of Your Life*, by Drs. Henry Cloud and John Townsend. These were some of the psychologists on the call-in show I told you about (in Chapter 1) that launched me into therapy. I began to pour through their book that is excellent. I learned that having boundaries is like a yard with a fence. We control the gate, who comes and goes, what comes in and goes out. Wow! This was a completely new concept for me. I could actually have some control over my own life? Life didn't have to just happen to me? I liked this idea. However, implementing this with people was another story altogether. The thought of it was frightening and seemed impossible. I hated even the thought of confrontation or conflict, or making other people angry with me. I would do anything to avoid conflict with other humans. In reality, doing *anything* for me meant I had frequent illness, depression, anxiety, and finally, this physical breakdown.

I've learned that people don't like it when you've always been a "yes" woman, and then, suddenly, you begin considering yourself and your schedule and saying "no" to their requests. I set a boundary with a friend who initially gave me the silent treatment. Later, she went off on me verbally. Finally, she sent her husband over to my home to berate me. You find out pretty quickly who your real friends are and who is only using you.

I had to grieve the people I was losing due to my new boundaries. Setting boundaries is very difficult at times and makes you question whether you're really doing the right thing. There were times I thought to myself, "Wait! Can I go back? This is too hard!" But, deep down inside me, I knew I wanted to be a confident woman in control of my own life and emotions. I wanted to be as "authentically me" as possible. I wanted what came out of my mouth to be true to what was in my heart. I wanted authenticity desperately, so I never gave up. I continued to learn how to put me, as well as my family, above other people, their families, activities, and institutions. Eventually, using boundaries and saying, "*no*" began to bring peace to my life. I was able to be there for my family more than I was there for the church, the school, anyone, anything. That felt truer to me.

It's amazing what I was able to accomplish once I learned to use boundaries to protect my time. I was learning to take personal responsibility for my life, for my time. I was learning how to leave other people's responsibilities to them, where they belonged. I was in control of my own life for the very first time! I was eventually able to use all my new free time to spend more time with my children, my little family. I had time to do nothing! I had time to read tons of parenting books, and self-help books recommended by my therapist. I began to enjoy playing with my children, enjoy my home, and enjoy my family. I mean, I don't know about you, but I think those things I just described above are more important than any other thing I could spend my time doing. They are priceless, precious, fleeting and… the most important things. I was able to calm down, finish school and start my private practice.

Setting boundaries helped me to begin to be present for *my own life*, and to be able to actually have a *life*. I began to love my life!

There is absolutely no way to be authentic and experience confidence without learning to use your voice to say what you need to say and to begin using your "no!" It was a life-changer for me.

YOU TEACH PEOPLE HOW TO TREAT YOU!

Having been dependent upon others liking me, upon others approving of me, and upon fitting in, when I set some boundaries, anger sometimes came from people whom I considered to be friends. My personal sense of worth was called onto the stage of life and it felt naked. Naked. Me. On. The. Stage. I had to scramble to find my self-worth. I had to choose myself, even if everyone else left me.

I'd have to go through this process every time I said "no" to someone. The first feeling that came was, "I don't deserve to be bold, to set boundaries, to speak my mind. Who do I think I am?" That was for those amazing speaker ladies at conferences. Not me. In the process, I was facing the challenges. Was I going to choose me over fitting in? Would I choose me over pleasing other people? Next, I would remember: "This is my chance to choose me and my life." I knew that deep inside. Ride or die. Step up or step back, forever. With the help of my therapist, and a few friends cheering me on, I was able to eventually step up for myself. I learned that by what I allowed to come into my life, I was teaching people how to treat me. I was facing the truth, living the truth, and saying the truth. More free time and peacefulness was the reward - the new normal.

Have you ever faced walking up many floors in a high rise? I live on the 19th floor. A few weeks ago, the elevators were out and we had to use the steps. The first three flights feel pretty good, and then, there are the other sixteen flights. I'm holding onto the railing at the bottom, breathing heavily, looking up the steps and saying to myself, "Sixteen more flights." That experience is exactly how I felt some days, processing, holding onto my boundaries, respecting my own voice, and loving myself enough to be authentic. I remember how I felt when I finally made it to the top of those nineteen flights: exhilaration, joy, accomplishment, sweet sweat and smiles! That's also how it felt to finally be there for myself. That's how I felt every time I was able to hold my ground and make the decision that was the best for me and my life.

I love this quote by Georgia O'Keeffe:

"I've been absolutely terrified every moment of my life, and I've never let it keep me from doing a single thing that I wanted to do."

Don't ever let fear hold you back. I've been there. If I can change, you can change. Many women have changed. It's possible. I promise. I won't promise it will be easy, but I can promise that, if you begin to implement boundaries, stand up for yourself, use your voice, and have your own life, it's totally worth all the initial pain. Find a therapist or a group of healthy people and allow them to support you while you learn how to say "no." Let them support you while you learn to love yourself and while you begin to matter to yourself.

JOURNAL PROMPTS

- Do you see yourself as a boundaryless, people-pleaser?

- Are you ready to find your "No!" and take back your life?

- Look at your current obligations. Do you like all of them or do these things bring you joy?

- Is there time left in your day for living your life? Or, like I did, do you feel your life is an endless string of groundhog days?

- If you quit taking responsibility for everyone else, what things might you finally have time to do?

Chapter 4

Frame the Shame - Speak
Your Secrets

*M*y newest client, had tender, light brown, child-like eyes that gazed only to the ground. My immediate sense was that she didn't yet have her self-confidence or trust in place to look me in the eyes as we shook hands. I welcomed her and led her into my small office in an older home in Hyde Park. It is pleasantly comfortable and homey, decorated in soft colors with splashes of light. Carrie kept her head down, still looking at the ground, but smiled gently as she sat on the edge of the couch.

Before my healing journey began, I didn't have any intuition. Well, I probably had it, it just didn't work or maybe I wasn't listening… I'm an empath, a highly sensitive person so sometimes my heart gets ahead of my brain, especially with people. My adult daughter, Elise, has said, 'Mom, you like everybody.' She's right LOL, I do really like, and love most people. When I see or meet people, I tend to see their soul. In other words, I see them in all their potential. I don't know how to explain it, but I know I'm not the only one who sees people this way because I've asked. Anyway, this way of seeing people used to get me into all kinds of trouble because even though people have potential, they don't always choose to live in it! So I had to spend some time working on being more willing to see their soul, and at the same time, evaluate where they are in the present time. A more balanced approach to seeing people.

My intuition has grown a great deal in recent years. Most times, I am able to read people pretty well. I get a feeling or a sense inside, and like a blanket of freshly fallen snow, a knowing seems to fall on me. Sometimes it falls like a wild snowstorm; other times, it falls like a soft, gentle snowfall. I remember the sense that came to me when I met Carrie. I sensed she was a beautiful heart, sensitive, very kind; and she also had suffered horrific abuse. I wanted to hold Carrie and say, "I see you! I see your pain without you saying one word. I don't know you yet, but I see you. And if you could see what I see, you would be awed, because it's so incredible! I can see that you are beautiful, powerful, unique, and deeply precious. You are going to be fine!" However, I knew from experience and my profession that my heartfelt, authentic words would not sink in at this point. I'd been where Carrie was that day - ashamed, confused, feeling broken and feeling maybe there wasn't really any hope, only SHAME.

I remember my first trip to my own therapist's office. I was terrified! I had a recurring nightmare that she'd look at me, and after a few minutes she would say, "Listen, honey. You are a mess that I can't begin to help. There really is no hope for you. Maybe you should get a bunch of cats and live your best life." LOL. Much to my surprise, she never said anything like that. I now know that, everyone who truly wants to get help, has 100% hope of healing.

Clearly, Carrie was feeling shame. She couldn't look up at me for most of the session. I am quite familiar with shame. With shame, you feel like, deep down in your soul, there is a darkness, a badness that everyone can see. You feel broken beyond repair, wounded beyond words. You're sure that, if anyone ever saw that part of you, they would run out of the room screaming. It doesn't matter what good other people tell you they see in you; you simply cannot believe their words. The words just cannot sink in because you're sure they would never say them if they really knew the real you. It's like your ears are made of Teflon. The words don't stick, they slide right off.

In recent years, it's as though I can see right inside people to the real, authentic person. To the naked eye, it can appear something quite the opposite. I could see this young woman was a bright light and brilliant, despite the bowed head and eyes staring at the ground, too ashamed to look up.

After working together for several weeks, I noticed Carrie began to look into my eyes. Her eyes said she was beginning to feel safe with me. She had begun to trust the process, and our therapeutic, authentic, and blooming relationship was helping her to see things she would never have imagined could be true.

While describing the abuse she suffered, Carrie would stare off and, as tears welled up in her eyes, she'd share with me bits and pieces of the horror she'd experienced in her childhood home. Sometimes she would be mid-sentence and I would notice a look of sheer terror in her eyes. Then she would move her eyes toward me, and I'd smile and remind her that she was now safe. "Carrie, right now, you are here in this room of safety with me. I won't let anything happen to you here. You are safe. Breathe with me." She would take in air and look into my eyes with the eyes of a little girl, although she was well into her thirties. I sensed she felt the safety envelop her as her countenance began to be peaceful. The pain she'd endured at the hands of her father, mother, and brother, almost on a daily basis, I could see was unbearable.

I could feel she began to have a seed of hope growing inside her. She kept working hard to believe that her abuse wasn't something she had done, that that wasn't who she was, and that it wasn't her fault—this is the SHAME. Instead, she learned, there was *something wrong and broken in her abusers*. These are reasons, not excuses. She was an innocent victim of her abusers' will and she was too young to understand. Her father and his friends abused Carrie sexually and filmed her for many years. Her abuse was horrific, one of the most heinous stories, in my career, that I've ever heard. Every once in a while, she would bring her eyes up to mine and, as a little child, she would ask, "Are you sure it's not my fault?" My heart would break open for Carrie. A compassion bigger than myself came right through my body - I believe this love to be God or Spirit. I wanted to hold that little girl part of her and never let her go.

From the ages of 2-18, all Carrie knew was being used and abused and filmed. Her father set up online meetings with older men, and forced her to comply. A couple of years into therapy, she began to understand that this wasn't her fault, and she began to have a spark of joy in her eyes and on her face! I felt such awe for her gift of healing. Carrie began feeling, maybe for the first time, that she truly was special and that she possessed great worth. She started doing loving self-care. Carrie is one of the most courageous, brave, and beautiful women, inside and out, with whom I have been honored to work. She sends me into AWE! She did the hard healing work, week after week. She said she was feeling alive again and that she would always love herself and choose herself from now on. One day Carrie came in and told me she was beginning to enjoy her artwork again! She began to truly live her life on her terms, without the demons of abusive memories hounding her every minute of every day.

Shame keeps us small, quiet and living in the background. It tells us that we are profoundly insignificant, unworthy of love, incapable of fitting into any type of community. There's a sense inside that you better stay small and invisible because if others get a glimpse into you, they will see what you see: darkness, a non-person, guilt, shame. There is a fear that if people see inside you, they will shriek in horror.

Shame keeps us in the house, on our couch, watching TV, playing video games, browsing social media, online shopping, and eating or drinking to excess, dragging ourselves out the door only long enough to get what we need to keep staying invisible in our home, with our TV, internet, games, and false comforts. TVs don't see us, games don't see us, food and drink don't see us, or talk back, or tell us what they see. They're just right there when we need them to escape our shame thoughts. They become our friends. We become obsessed with them. We escape into another world and our brains and painful feelings go on autopilot or numb.

I remember when I was trying to stay invisible while avoiding my feelings, watching reality TV with my pasta and cheese. OOOOOOhhh, I felt safe and free (not really) for a few hours, just comforting myself. However, it always ended. Those feelings of worthlessness and insignificance would creep right back. I would try to cover them up with makeup, hair straightener, a new, cute top. I tried. But those feelings of shame were always there to remind me, no matter what, "You are never going to be okay."

Even while I was laughing, it would hit me with, "Be careful. Don't let yourself be too happy right now because those bad feelings are the real thing…they're just a thought away."

I was on the bench of life. Dreams? What dreams? I remember thinking, "There must be exceptional people who get to dream, who get to think about soaring in life, rather than worrying about how to make it through the current day." That's where I was, just trying to survive the day.

There was always a mustard seed of hope though. While I felt stuck in trying to survive, there was always a seed of hope. Even if I thought the universe was only tolerating me, I had little sense or vision of confidence that someday, maybe, I would be one of those people who would feel like living life to the fullest. I remember taking baths at night in the winter to warm up. I'd read a book about how to be a good mom and I'd lose myself in the writer's words and life. I would think, "She's so smart and she seems to have her life together. I want to be like that. I want to feel that I'm okay enough to enjoy life. I can do things. I can dream of doing more." Sadly, I seemed to consistently come back to, "not me, not really." Shame is relentless.

Shame was a bully, continually reminding me that, deep down, I was worthless. In a pioneering study, psychologist and University of Texas professor, James Pennebaker, and his colleagues, studied what happened when trauma survivors, specifically, rape and incest survivors, kept their experiences secret. We survivors fear telling anyone what happened to us because they may end up feeling about us the way we feel about ourselves. They may see the shame inside us. They may reject us. Shame keeps us on the sidelines of life, alone with our feelings of worthlessness. No one talks about this stuff. We smile, dress ourselves up for the day, and pretend all is good, or we hide in our beds and shut the world out. But we don't talk about it. I didn't talk about it for 30 years. The research team found that the act of not discussing traumatic events, of confiding in another person, could be more damaging than the actual event. Conversely, when people shared their stories and experiences, their physical health improved, their doctor visits decreased, and they showed significant decreases in their stress hormones.

We have to start talking out loud about sexual abuse, sexual assault, any and all trauma we've experienced, with someone safe. Imagine when you have a stomach virus and you finally throw up. (sorry to be gross, it's just such a good example LOL) You begin to feel better suddenly, right? You're lying on your bed or couch, you feel human again, the nausea is gone. It's a gross analogy, yes. However, it's a perfect analogy for when we tell a safe person, someone with empathy, what has happened to us. We immediately feel relief, we feel almost more human again. For me, I realized I was not alone. Millions of other women have felt like I felt. It's actually frightening how many of us women have experienced some type of sexual harassment, assault, rape, and we tell no one ever! The stats say 1 of 4, but I swear if we took a recount and people were honest, it's more like 1 of 2. Telling my kind, accepting therapist, I began to feel like, for the first time, I was becoming free of the shackles of the dark secrets of the abuse and the lies that said my abuse was my fault.

It's so important to know the difference between shame and guilt. Shame comes inside us as a result of abuse and trauma. Shame is not guilt. I want you to understand the difference. Guilt is, "I did something I feel bad about" or, "I did something wrong" or, "My behavior was wrong." When we feel guilt, we can own it;

we can make amends, if need be. Shame is put on us by others or ourselves. Shame is the sidekick of abuse. The shame gremlins come into our heads and begin to terrorize us with thoughts of what a horrible, evil person we must be to have been abused. See how twisted that is? Shame is, "I am bad, and wrong and worthless, and I AM my bad behavior." See the difference?

How do we get rid of this shame that spreads like black paint on a white tile floor throughout our soul? First, we find a safe place and a safe person with whom to share our abuse story. We bring the shame out of the darkness or secret place and bring it into the light, sharing our story with a trusted friend or therapist. In telling a trusted and trained therapist, you will be redirected to see the truth: you were not responsible for what another human chose to do with the power he/she had over you. We learn that, with support, we can untangle and unpack all of the trauma and learn to recognize our triggers for feeling shame. We learn to put the blame where it belongs, rather than blaming ourselves. Then, we practice this shame resilience every day. The more we learn about shame, the less shame will assault us! The more we talk about the feelings and effects of shame, the more shame disappears. Two excellent books to get you started on the healing path for shame are, Healing The Shame That Binds You, by John Bradshaw, and Daring Greatly, by Brene' Brown.

Another piece of shame resilience, for me, personally, is quiet, grounding time. Doctors tell us to work out for at least 30 minutes per day, 5-7 days per week, to keep our bodies healthy. Why not also set aside a certain amount of time for our hearts, minds and souls to be healthy? I began a practice years ago that has transformed my life. I get up early most days and spend one to two hours with me. I made a space with a comfy chair, a table and lamp, and a basket for my books and journals. I get a cup of coffee and I do several things, not in any particular order. I feel for what I want or need to do for me. If I need to release feelings, I write them in my journal. It doesn't have to be any certain way. It's just me sharing my feelings and processing through them. I may decide to listen to meditation music, or to meditate. There are meditation videos on YouTube, and www.fragrant-heart.com has hundreds of free meditations that you may search by topic. Meditation has been recognized by scientists as a wonderful healing agent for trauma and abuse. Another practice I do is to read books that will help me get to the next level of healing. There's no one way to spend time with yourself. The only requirement is making the commitment that you are worthy of time with yourself.

Quiet, grounding time is the part of the day I reserve especially for my mind, soul, and heart—the real me. I treasure it. When you first begin this practice, it can be daunting to sit still. Don't make it difficult or judge yourself or set ridiculous standards for what it needs to be (can you tell I did this in the beginning LOL?). Just spend time with yourself and your higher power, if that brings you comfort. You get to plan how your time is going to be. Alone time can be very healing. You get to spend time getting to know your interesting self! I know that sounds strange, but truly most people don't have any idea who they are, really. I know I didn't.

This daily practice has been key to learning how to have a relationship with myself and how to love myself. For many years, stemming from the abuse, I hated myself, loathed myself. This hatred made me do self-destructive things and self-sabotage-y things. It contributed to my depression and anxiety. Once I began to have quiet time every day, I slowly began to get to know the real me. I began to be kind to me. I began to have compassion for the part of me that went through all the abuses and traumas. I eventually began to love myself well. I promise you, if you're feeling there's no way you will ever love yourself, trust me. I felt this way. I thought, "Maybe that can happen for other women, but I don't think I could ever love me." Again, if someone like me can change, I know you can, too. There's always hope. I was so lost and hopeless for myself to ever be in the place I am in now: happy, healthy, joyful, free of the gremlins and the intrusive thoughts and memories. Forever, free!

Another good practice is to be aware of your own self-talk, the constant conversation that goes on inside everyone. My first therapist, Meg, asked me to keep track of the things I say to myself in private. At first, I remember thinking, "I don't think I talk to myself in private." However, once I began to observe my constant conversation within myself, I was shocked. Your self-talk can consist of your own criticism and hatred as well as your parents', grandparents', teachers', coaches' and co-workers' past or present criticisms. It's a very interesting exercise to tease out all the people we've agreed with to criticize ourselves.

I started to write down phrases I would hear myself say. For example, after leaving a conversation with someone, I would hear, "What the heck were you thinking, and why did you say that? You sounded like a total idiot. You'd be better off keeping your big mouth shut!" If I'd pass a window or mirror, I'd hear, "What did you wear that for? What made you think you looked okay in this outfit? You are so fat! You are so ugly, Cindy!" I could go on and on. The beauty of observing yourself is that, once you are aware of your self-talk, you can begin to change it.

Self-awareness is a catalyst for change!

I know it sounds like a lot of work, practicing everyday how to change your self-talk and learning to love yourself. But, I can't tell you how much it changes everything! Why wouldn't you and I be worth time spent, practicing and becoming a loving, loyal friend to ourselves? I've always been perplexed at how I spent 7 years at school, practicing becoming a good therapist and coach. But, no time or education is required to become a functioning adult in our society. No time or education is necessary to bring a human into the world and raise them. No time or education is required to be in a marriage with another human. How bizzare! Have you ever thought about that? Some of the most important things we'll ever do—yet we do zero preparation? Crazy! You are worth some time and some education to be fulfilled and content in your life.

I practiced every day, and I remember thinking, "If I ever spoke to my friends like I speak to myself, I wouldn't have any friends. No one would put up with this abuse!" I began to notice when I criticized myself. I would turn it around and change the words to words I would say to my own children or to my friends. It was weird at first, but it truly has helped me. After practicing this for a number of years, I genuinely know, deep in my heart and soul, that I am worthy of my own love and the love of other people, including my higher power. I no longer tolerate myself or other people speaking to me in a negative way. Today, I don't listen to hateful, abusive critical words from anyone. I walk away.

JOURNAL PROMPTS:

- Is it time for you to share your story with a trusted friend or therapist?

- When you read the part on shame, how did that resonate with you? Are you possibly feeling shame from your experience with abuse or maybe childhood in general?

- How do you think having a daily practice of your own might help you feel more connected with yourself?

- Have you ever observed your self-talk? Are you happy with it currently? What are some practical steps could you take to change it?

Chapter 5

Compassion for Yourself

Kelsey's story-

*S*ummers, as a child at my grandparents' farm, were magical! There were horses, a pony, tire swings hanging from huge, magnificent oak trees and green pastures that went on as far as the eye could see. Dogs, cats, and my very cool, older, teen cousin lived there. I stayed for a week or two almost every summer. I loved my cousin. She spent a lot of time with me. I watched her put on her makeup and curl her hair for hours. She would put makeup on me and paint my nails. She taught me everything I ever knew about makeup, and boys, and I thought she was so cool because, although she was my cousin, she was only a little less than a decade older than me.

My family spent many Sunday afternoons and holidays at my grandparents' farm. That farm was the place I felt I belonged, along with all my dad's siblings and their children. As a child, I felt we all belonged to each other and it was a community that had a revered place in my young heart. On Sundays, my cousin and I would be so excited to set the huge, sprawling table set for at least 30 or so of us, especially once we made it to the adult table. I never did like being made to sit at the kids' table in the kitchen. I was always afraid I would miss something. And, now I know I missed a lot, sitting at that kids' table. I'm winking at you. The adults conversing about adult stuff was always much more intriguing!

There was a huge oak tree in the back field. I would go out in the mornings and swing on the tire swing by myself with the crickets, all chirping in unison. The farm was so quiet in the summers. I could escape into another world there. I could imagine being anyone and I remember pretending to live in that beautiful garden-like place. I loved being away from the busyness of my suburb home. I loved being with my cousins. I loved being away from my own chaotic, somewhat noisy home and my siblings.

However, I began to realize there were dark secrets there on that farm. As a child, I always hoped the secret stuff would end. I desperately wanted to believe they would go away and that things would change. They didn't. My grandmother was not your typical grandma—as in kind and sweet, baking cookies. As I think about her now, she was a very unhappy woman, and my cousins and I used to try to avoid her. She was somewhat mean-spirited, and argumentative. As an adult, I can look back and recognize she was a mix of angry, controlling, committed fundamentalist, and pious. She felt she was superior in knowledge to everyone. She would argue with anyone who would take her on. She would squint her beady eyes, glare and shout argumentative words at my aunts and uncles, at repairmen that came by, at grocery store cashiers, at anyone, really. She would shout about the Bible, about God. She could be quite aggressive. I don't remember ever not feeling a little afraid in her presence. She wasn't the kind of grandma who was going to rock me to sleep, hold me tenderly, and read me fairytales. She appeared to be a strong woman and she felt it was her mission to teach people everything they didn't know. In her own mind I think she saw herself as God's right hand woman or something.

One day she ordered my cousin and me into the car without explanation. We looked at each other with wonder and concern because she never took us anywhere without our older cousin, Nicky. We were a little scared, but too afraid to ask. Grandma sternly drove up to the white double doors of a tiny country church. As she pulled up, she told us to "go on, get out," and said, "Go watch the movie, and I'll be back to pick you up." I remember feeling strange walking into an unknown church alone. We were just little kids, maybe only 9 or 10 years old. We didn't know anybody. We walked in slowly, with our eyes open wide, not really sure what to expect. The church was full. We had to sit near the front, never anticipating what would happen next. The lights went down and the room became dark. I grabbed Shannon's hand and she grabbed mine. Suddenly, light appeared on a screen above the pool where they baptized people.

A movie called, *The Gates of Hell!* began to play. It was a horror flick, just like the title says. We both put our hands over our eyes. When we peeked out, there were scenes of people dying from motorcycle accidents, car accidents, shootings, drug use and many others. The main characters once dead, instantly found themselves in a place called "Hell." The scenes in Hell would shift from worms crawling out of their eyes, ears, and noses, eating their flesh, to a constant fire that burned them alive. In this Hell, the characters never died. They suffered these tortures over and over for infinity. They wailed in pain and horror. The shrill screams went through our little bodies like metal on metal. The movie ended and the fat little preacher ran up to the podium that he could barely see over and said, "If you don't want to go to Hell when you die," then he paused…"then you better come up here and let someone lead you to Christ right now! Now is the time to get right with God!" We were terrified. Both my cousin and I, soaked with our terror tears, ran up to the front of the church, arm in arm. We were taking no chances on ending up in the horrible place we witnessed, called Hell. We filled out a little white card with our information. A woman with big hair prayed over us. We figured we signed ourselves right out of Hell. Or so we thought.

Grandma was a "shame keeper." She was the matriarch of the family. She determined what was good for everyone in the family, and the family acquiesced. I remember being a skinny little kid. My cousin and I were making white toast joyfully one afternoon, with lots of melted butter on it. Grandma walked in and said, "You're going to be as fat as your mother!" I looked down at my skinny body and thought, for the first time ever, "Am I fat?" That was the beginning of my issues with body image and food. Grandma lectured like it was her happy place. She lectured anytime she had the opportunity. She was had a sharp tongue, and her mindset was definitely scarcity. She lectured us about getting fat, about eating food, about God and His wrath to come. She even argued with us about coloring inside the coloring book lines. I used to believe God was like Grandma, maybe just a little worse, if that was possible.

I remember feeling a desire to stay clear of her. I had one good grandma, so I knew what good grandmas were like, and she was not one of them. She shamed me for many things over the years. I didn't recognize it at the time, but her shaming words were burrowing in through my skin, right into my little young heart. Shame stings deep inside. Her words, over the years, made the real me shrink down inside myself, little by little. This Grandma would have been a walk in the park compared to the other hells there on the farm. The worst part, I realized once I was an adult, was that she kept these family secrets and used religion to cover over them.

Grandma's secrets involved sexual abuse. This went on for many years, on her watch. There were many of my aunts, uncles, and cousins who were abused. Our souls were forever tethered with sexual shame. There was the aunt who regularly told us as children, the details of her sexual encounters. I was 8 or 9 years old. I listened, although reluctantly, so she would like me and think I was cool. I thought the sun rose and set on my aunt. She was very hip and she was kind to me and I loved her deeply. Honestly, I was too young to understand the things she would share with me. I certainly didn't know what intercourse was, or an erection, much less what ejaculation meant. But she made sure I had all the details. We didn't talk about sex in our family, no one did really. I was left to my own imagination. Therefore, my grandparents' home became a place with many dark secrets that I wouldn't dare tell my parents. I carried deep shame about this for years.

I don't remember how old I was when the sexual abuse began. I didn't want to let these experiences taint my love for my grandfather. I learned to ignore the memories and deny it was ever happening. I believed it would go away someday and life would be back to normal. This carried on through several generations. No one ever mentioned it. Eventually, in my thirties, I had to talk about the abuse and the shame. That's when I began my work with Cindy.

End of Kelsey's Story

Kelsey's story is a common one in my work. When you see the memes that say, "Be kind to everyone, because everyone has pain they don't talk about," it's true. Beautiful, intelligent, amazing women walk into my office every week and tell me story after story, just like this one. The settings may be different, but the resulting destruction of pain and shame is the same.

In the years leading up to my therapy in my late twenties, my own sexual assault was not only in my subconscious. I was feeling shame, and feeling intense guilt. Always at the front of my mind was the fear of being attacked or "over-taken." This is one reason, I believe, I always cowered to loud people and avoided conflict at all costs. This resulted in people-pleasing. I hated conflict. My basic premise was "just tell me what I need to do to make you stop yelling or upset and make you happy with me." This is how my love for humor developed. If I could make people laugh, then they were too happy to pull me into conflict or to yell at me. The fear I developed was debilitating. I was convinced I would feel this way forever.

Through enduring my own sex abuse, I became hyper vigilant, suspicious, a fast walker, analyzing strangers in parking lots and malls. My sisters used to joke and call me "the detective." I thought that was just my personality. I had no idea that it was my trauma rearing its ugly head. As a result of the trauma, I reacted at a level "10" for things that someone else without trauma might react at a level "2." It was embarrassing. I, like the people around me, was shocked and baffled by some of my reactions. My fear and anxiety was off the charts and I was unable to hide it. I remember having nightmares every single night. Many times, religion was used to shame me for my nightmares. I was told, "Maybe you're having nightmares because you should feel guilty about something you've done." This person was implying that God was giving me nightmares because he was trying to get through to me the guilt I should feel about my sin. I was already so broken inside, and then God was brought in to slam the gavel down on the table, declaring my guilt, too! I'd been violated by adults who should have loved and cared for me, but instead, they hurt me. I felt unworthy deep inside, full of crushing shame. I felt like it was my fault, like I actually brought on this abuse. Religious and emotional abuse can be devastating to the mind.

The result of being shamed in that way, for me, was a sense of inherent badness. By the time I was a teenager, I felt such shame inside, I truly didn't care what happened to me. I began drinking at 13 years old. I loved being drunk because, when I was drunk, I didn't have to feel anything. I became a risk taker. I didn't care about my life and preserving it. I remember crying as softly as possible into my pillow at night. I felt so sad, and yet, I didn't want anyone to hear me. I felt at times like a swirling drain was inside me pulling me down into a dark hole and felt so alone. I sometimes wondered if I was going to be lost someplace and I'd never find my way back. Eventually, I became somewhat unaware of myself—I was dissociating (a common coping mechanism of trauma). I had disappeared to some other place and I was just acting out the motions of my life. I don't remember ever feeling truly happy or safe.

I developed in the ninth grade, my jeans were a size 6 and my bra size began at a size "DD." This brought such attention from the boys, and male teachers I'm sorry to say. Wandering eyes, jokes. The shame seemed to increase for me within this body. When I became a part of the popular group in high school, I was approached by the older boys and didn't have a clue how to set boundaries. I didn't believe I was valuable enough to deserve boundaries. The abuse left me unable to value myself enough to believe I was worth protecting. However, I had learned very well by high school to act and wear an "I'm normal and happy" mask. I remember one of my male teachers smiling and asking me, "Cindy, you're just happy go lucky, aren't you?" I smiled back as if to agree, but I felt anything but "happy go lucky" inside. I actually felt like I was dying inside. My spirit and soul were in agony. I would get drunk every weekend and imitate people to make my friends laugh. I was the life of the party.

The "happy go lucky" was just a cover-up for my deep, dark pain.

As I ponder my young adult years, married with three children by the age of 27, I was still giving off the "happy go lucky" impression. I thought that was what I was supposed to do. Don't feel. Just pretend. Don't feel anything. Present a happy mom, a Christian, the mask of a sweet, quiet, un-opinionated woman. When I think of the caldron of rage that was boiling beneath the surface of myself inside my belly, I don't know how I covered it so well. People would say to me, "Cindy, you're so sweet." I'd think to myself, "If you only knew." Eventually, that rage would boil over and spill out all over my life. During my sophomore year of high school, a guy friend I thought I knew well had me over to hang out. It was a Saturday afternoon and it wasn't unusual for Mike and me to hang out and drink together before going out. I drove over to Mike's house. When he answered the door, I was happy to hear him say his parents were out of town for the weekend. That meant we could drink and listen to music openly. We began listening to a Def Leppard album he'd bought earlier that day. Def Leppard was one of my favorite bands at the time. I was really getting into the music and enjoying talking with Mike about the look of the new album. In the 80's, albums were like 16"x16" with works of art. When a new album came out, we couldn't wait to check out the band's cover, and the new songs' lyrics typed right on the albums inner cover!

After a few beers, Mike sat down next to me on the floor. That wasn't unusual. However, the way he looked at me felt strange. I stood up and sat on the brown leather couch, although I wasn't feeling in any way that I was unsafe. Mike and I had hung out many times together alone, and other times, with friends, over the years. I felt safe with him. My logical brain was overriding my intuitional gut, and I remember telling myself I was just imagining what my gut was trying to warn me about.

Not listening to our gut feelings is so dangerous. I've talked to so many women, just like me. They didn't listen to their gut when it told them to run. Suddenly, Mike whipped around, up on the couch by me and came in as if he were going to kiss me. I laughed, pushed him, and said, "Stop it, Mike. You're such a dork!" in a playful tone. I was trying to fend off his approach with humor and banter as I wondered if he was just playing. "Surely, he is playing," I thought. It was such unusual behavior for him. Surely, I'm crazy for thinking he's serious. What's happening? I still was not really feeling too afraid. He was my friend. Surely, he knew that I wasn't going to have sex with him. For goodness sake, I was dating one of his friends! He laughed and sat down and took a drink of his beer. Mike was a big guy, one of the players on our high school football team. He was a huge guy with big muscles, very good-looking. But I'd never imagined more than a friendship with him. For me, the chemistry just wasn't there. I began wondering, after he did try to kiss me, would I enjoy this type of interaction with him? "No," I thought, "he's not my type."

Suddenly, I noticed that his gaze changed, and I realized he was serious. Again, he came toward me and forced his lips onto mine. Now I was scared and began to feel pissed. "What the hell!" I thought to myself. "This is crazy!" Humor and laughter weren't working. He had me pinned on the couch and was all over me, feeling all over my body through my clothing and looking into my eyes with this determined look. I looked him in the eyes and screamed, "Get off of me!!!" I was still holding out hope that he was kidding and would stop. I loved my friend. I didn't want us not to be friends. Why was he doing this? What brought this about? Is this my fault?

Did I lead him on? Did I come across like I was interested in more with him? My mind was spinning with thoughts and questions and guilt. Finally, I began to realize I had to fight him. He wasn't letting up. He was much stronger than I was. I began to be scared to death. I began thinking he could rape me if he wanted because I could feel he was so much stronger than me. No one was home. He was so strong I wasn't able to budge him off. I fought and struggled, and it was clear to me he had the upper hand. I was not going to get out of this. He began to go under my gray, hooded sweatshirt and feel my breasts. I felt disgusted. He put his hand down my pants and began to touch me. I was so scared. I kept screaming and fighting. He didn't care. Suddenly, we heard the front door slam shut, and our friend, Dan, called out Mike's name. Mike jumped off of me.

He got up, pulled himself together and went out of the room to Dan in the foyer. He acted like nothing had happened! I was left in his family room, a complete wreck of emotions and disbelief. I pulled my clothes together, fixed my hair and went out where they were drinking beer and talking at the kitchen table. I didn't know what to do. I was shaking and walking toward the front door when Dan yelled, "Hey, Cindy, where are you going?" Without responding, I went out to my car, started it, and sped away. I began to sob. The tears were so thick I could hardly see to drive. I remember feeling dazed and confused, completely grossed out. Why did he put his hands all over me? What just happened? Did it really happen? Am I having a bad nightmare? Was it my fault? What did I do to cause this behavior? I know now that I did nothing, absolutely nothing. I sometimes wondered if I had a sticker on my head that said, "Use and abuse me, it's okay!" I began to beat myself up inside: "You can't even keep your sexual-self hidden when you need to!" Or, "You ruined a great friendship." Or, "Why did you wear makeup? Why that shirt? Why did you curl your hair?" I vacillated between beating myself up and blaming myself and wondering what the hell was wrong with Mike. I never told a soul. Mike and I never spoke of it and never again were we friends even though we were in the same high school group, and I had to see him every weekend. We would catch each other's eye accidently, but I'd look away quickly. The shame kept me quiet. I felt like my gut-GPS was busted, and I believed these things were all my fault.

One weekend that same year, my best friend's parents were out of town, and as always, we were planning the biggest, best party ever! Her home was up a long private drive and there was plenty of land around it, so we didn't have to worry about the music being loud or neighbors seeing our friend's cars. We were on our own and her parents were always gone. We made sure everyone who mattered knew about the party, planned for the alcohol, etc. All of us girls decided to meet an hour early to have a few beers. We were laughing, telling stories about the week, when we heard the back door open. I remember thinking "it's our friends," but I suddenly realized a group of guys we didn't know had somehow found out about the party and just randomly showed up. They started coming in with their cases of beer, loud, roudy, kinda rude and we were a little taken aback. We weren't sure what to do. None of us even thought about dialing 911 and saying there are strange men in our house…we just sat there waiting to see what would happen, while they sat on the couches in her great room…we weren't sure what to do, who they were or how to handle any of it really. As I look back now, I think just how very dangerous this scenario was. One of the guys commented on someone's "tits" and how large and amazing they looked. My friends and I became scared… it was one thing to have strange guys in the house, but now they were being dark and aggressive as hell. As all the guys looked at each other in a way that said, "Let's do this!" Then they got up and came towards our table of friends. This could have been a major disaster if our guy friends hadn't walked in at the exact same time. A fight broke out and our football player friends were able to fight these random guys and get them to leave the house.

Sexual assault is real. There really are men who think women and their bodies are objects to be used and they have cart blanche to have control over women. Women are people, with feelings, and lives and just because we happen to be in these amazing, beautiful, sexy bodies—doesn't mean we are objects. Just because you admire how our bodies are shaped, and they turn you on, doesn't give you the right to them! Why has this behavior and sense of ownership not changed much over the centuries? Why do we women sometimes feel it's our fault that some men stare at us, and feel they have a right to our bodies? WHERE is the training and education for men around women's bodies and sexual assault? It's basically, NOWHERE!

When are your sisters, wives, daughters, friends going to be important enough for people to make a stand against sexual assault? There are many of us women who, by the time of our high school years, have experienced one or more sexual assaults or attempts. Our stories are all different in that it may have been a family member, a neighbor, a church leader, an uncle, a family friend, a boyfriend, a girlfriend's brother, a grandfather, or all of the above - but the results are very much the same. We are in shock and disbelief. We suffer post-traumatic pain, shame, and debilitating loss in selfesteem as a result. Isn't that ironic? We are the victims of the abusers, yet we feel responsible. Maybe that has something to do with the way we call women "sluts" if they have sex with many partners by consent, but guys get a slap on the back and a "high-five" for sleeping around. "Way to go, dude!" It's infuriating. Why two different responses to the same thing? I was hoping that ended in my generation, but "slut shaming" women is alive and well in society. The 2019 Bachelorette, Hannah Brown, was slut shamed by a man who was unhappy with her decision to have sex with one of the bachelors before marriage. Who was he to judge her life and decisions? We women need to stop being "nice" and "quiet" and putting up with this double standard.

In society, we have numerous teen pregnancies each year. Every time, for generations, everyone says, "OOOOOH MYYYYYY," and they cover their mouths and their eyes bulge out, signaling, "What is this? What have you done?" Seriously, the last thing a 15-year-old pregnant girl needs is to be shamed and judged. She needs love, support, and people around her, saying, "We got you!" I'm pretty sure the percentage of teens who really want to be pregnant hovers around zero.

We often blame ourselves for sexual assault, and society endorses the blame, with judgments like: "She shouldn't have been wearing the short skirt or low-cut blouse. She was asking for it! She just looks slutty!" I'm here to tell you, no woman who has experienced sexual assault ever wanted to be assaulted. It's not the clothes, it's not the looks. It's generations of patriarchal misogyny coupled with our society and our government not taking sexual crimes against women seriously. Objectification of women is so commonplace that the majority of even women don't notice. I assure you, it's alive and well. Not one of us who have had to endure a man's unwanted, disgusting hands all over our bodies against our will, or who have been forced to have sex, wanted it. NONE OF US! For me, my work in therapy was to realize that what happened to me doesn't define me. What happened to me was the act of will of another human being. I didn't cause the assault. I didn't ask for the assault. I didn't deserve the assault. The deeper question was, "Who is going to make it better for me?"

There was only one answer to that question-- "Me." I was the one who had to go to therapy. I was the one who had to unlearn all the things I came to believe about myself as a result of assault. I had to unlearn the shame, worthlessness, fearfulness, boundarylessness. I had to practice, day after day, to be kind to myself by having compassion, to learn to see myself as worthy and valuable, and to advocate for me to all the gremlins in my head. My pain was not my fault, but it was 100% my responsibility. If I remained a *victim* of the abuse, I would have probably become addicted to something, and I would have perpetuated more victim-ness and abuse in my life. That's how it goes. Generation after generation of some women teach girls to be quiet, shy, unopinionated, good, sweet. And the rapes continue. Yes, you read correctly. Some of us women are part of the problem. Many women, (maybe a higher percentage of religious women) still raise their girls to be these culture-induced robots of sticky sweet, submissive, rule followers. Silence. Mother's silence is also a part of the problem. It's tough to have these conversations, I get it, but if we don't have the difficult conversations with our daughters and their friends, look at the results! Look at the repercussions for us and for our daughters, sisters, friends! We have to stop! We have to tell our girls, "Yes, be as feminine as you are, but know that feminine is also loud, boundaried, empowered and strong." Feminine is loving yourself. We women are beasts! We run companies. We grow humans in our bodies. We push those humans out into the world! We raise families. We have to acknowledge the strength inside all of us as women. We have to pass that onto the future, female generations. We are powerful! We have to be powerful in a society that objectifies women's bodies.

Healing was no easy task, but I was determined. Victims cannot own their power until they willfully take it back from their abusers. For me, the way to take my power back was to diligently have compassion for my broken parts and to learn to love myself, authentically. I remember when I first set out to love myself, I mistakenly thought it was mani-pedis, hair, clothing, etc. I've learned that it's way more personal and way more deep than that. Selflove isn't an arrogant, conceited, phony thing. *Authentically loving me* meant changing the ways in which I thought about myself, spoke to myself, took care of my feelings, and gave myself permission to feel EVERYTHING. Acknowledging my feelings was the first step. I began feeling my feelings and caring for them like I would care for a newborn baby, day after day, night after night. I consistently had to stop allowing others to treat me poorly. I had to take time to be alone, time for therapy, time for feeling and processing my feelings. I had to begin by respecting myself.

After some years of daily, minute-by-minute practice in loving and caring for myself, I began to feel better. This is a journey, not a sprint, and it takes a lifetime of practice. This self-love thing is a daily practice, just like physically working out. Day in and day out, making choices that serve you best. It's not easy, but it is worth it.

Once I began to feel better about myself, and worked my therapy and processed most of my past pain, I was able to think about the next step for me. The next step was to recognize my trauma reactions, my angry outbursts, my boiling angry caldron, my edgyhardness toward abusers, my bitterness toward my perpetrators, seeking to control my husband, my kids, and others because of my out-of-control fear. The list goes on and on. I call this "traumadrama." Although I didn't cause my trauma, these behaviors were a result of my trauma, and they were all my responsibility to heal.

I had to own the pain I had inadvertently brought onto others. Ugh. This was difficult. It was quite difficult because when you're in your victim-ness, you feel really defensive when receiving feedback or correction. You feel somehow that you deserve to get away with trauma-drama. "After all I've been through, you're going to hold me accountable?!? How dare you?" That's really how it feels. After what I've been through, I have to control myself? Once I began to own that my trauma-drama had spilled onto others that I loved dearly, the owning began to feel good and right. I no longer felt such guilt or shame around how I had behaved. I owned it and began to change my behaviors. I had to continue to work to heal my own feelings. Honestly, the work never really ends. It's part of being a responsible human being. I'll get deeper into that in the next chapter.

There were things I remembered around hurting my loved ones with my rigid and prickly actions. I would acknowledge it, own it and apologize. I told my adult children, "When you remember, and you will remember, things I did or said that hurt you when I was in that headspace, please know you are welcome to come to me. I will own what I need to. I will help pay for your therapy." My kids have been so forgiving and gracious. I know how lucky I am and I 'm very grateful. They tell me I was a good mom, and I appreciate that. Over time I was able to own the things I'd done well, also. However, we all know there were times my trauma-drama caused them pain and their pain matters, too. It's been freeing to own and admit my mistakes, and to make amends, forgive myself, and respect myself. This is all part of the self-love journey.

JOURNAL PROMPTS

- Where are you still being quiet, unopinionated, and sweet, but a boiling cauldron of anger, underneath? Are you ready to be healed? You are amazing, I promise!

- What do you need to do? What do you need to feel? Do you need to begin to trust your own gut again? Do you know where to start?

- Is there pain you may need to heal? Is there anything stopping you from reaching out to a coach or therapist who is trauma capable?

Chapter 6

Acknowledge Your Grief

I walked back into the therapy office one day, after some months break from regular therapy, I sat down, and in frustration, I said, "I don't know what's going on with me." Immediately, as I got the words out, my eyes welled up and tears began to pour down. There were waves of tears crashing all over her office because I was feeling such intense pain. "Why am I here? Why am I this sad again? I'm so sick of feeling this way! I just want to be done with the crying and sadness! How much more time do I have to spend dealing with this pain? Shouldn't someone else have to take responsibility for this? I didn't do these things to hurt myself. Someone else did."

I was falling into a pit of despair and feeling like a victim. I hate feeling like a victim more than anything. I felt weak and stuck. I wanted to be free from crying, free from feeling like a mess.

I looked up, through the tears, and glanced at my therapist. She was loving and accepting, and her kind eyes were looking at me, as a mom who cares deeply for her daughter's feelings would. I knew deep down, that if I would simply allow myself to feel the feelings that were pulsing in my throat and let myself cry as hard and long as I needed to, she would help me get to a place of understanding.

I stopped crying and began to breathe enough that I could speak and said, "It's just that I cry—a lot. I feel like an idiot because I cry so much, even though I've pretty much worked through all my past hurts. So, it doesn't make sense that I feel this way. When will this pain end? Or is this what the rest of my life is going to look like? I feel lonely. I've chosen to take a break from some of my family and friends because of boundary issues, feeling judged, and I need support. Now that I'm making new choices and working to be more authentic, why do I feel more alone than ever? Before I made these boundary changes, at least I had a group or tribe I belonged to, even if it could be somewhat toxic."

Cheryl looked at me with compassion and said, "Cindy, you are beginning to grieve." Grieve? Why would I be grieving? Isn't grieving for people who've lost loved ones to death?

"Cindy, you are grieving many things of your past: the abuse, the lack of emotional support. Humans need to be seen and heard and validated. You needed to be loved and accepted unconditionally. You needed to feel safe as a little girl. You needed guidance and support. You needed to be able to be a little child and know that everything was going to be okay. All of these are a part of healthy nurturing that every child desperately needs. All the pain you dug up and worked to overcome in therapy, now needs to be grieved. This is a process. I promise. You won't feel this way forever."

"But, Cheryl," I said, "there are so many worse things people have been through in their lives, why is my life requiring so much work?"

"It's simple, Cindy. We don't have to win the contest for having the most pain on the planet in order to grieve our pain. Pain causes hurt feelings. Losing what we thought were close relationships with family/friends… it's brutal, but we have to honor ourselves and our right to be respected. Yes, some stories of pain are more horrific than others, but that doesn't cancel out our own. You are grieving. Grieving won't go on like this forever, but it will need to be acknowledged and felt from time to time."

"Yes," I thought, "she's right. This does feel like grief about loss." Finally, I could at least identify my deep feeling of sadness. For the first time, I realized my tears weren't telling me I needed to do more exploring or digging. I didn't need more therapy. I just needed to let the tears and grief come, feel the feelings, and give myself the love and care and patience that I needed. It was okay. I was okay. I just needed time. I felt a sense of relief come over my body. I didn't need more pain exploration. I needed to let myself feel sad about the fact that little me didn't have all she needed to feel good about herself, and now adult me will make sure to get all of that for myself.

Grieving over your losses in life is a lot like grieving when someone you love passes away. It's shocking when you first hear the news, you're in a bit of denial for a while, then you're sad, and finally, you begin to accept that all people die, eventually. This is a real part of life. You begin to accept that you will have to do life without your loved one who passed. This is acceptance of what is true. My work now was grieving that there were people I loved but was losing. And grieving the times I felt afraid as a little girl, that I endured abuse alone in ways that hurt me, and that I was lonely because I hadn't quite found a new tribe. I needed to accept that all of this was a part of my past. I needed to take responsibility for it instead of remaining a victim. I had a choice. The choice I made was to take responsibility instead of wallowing in being a victim. This choice was going to save my life and allow me to prosper, heal and move forward to complete empowerment.

I found that my grief ran deeper than just my past abuse. I began to grieve for the ways I'd loved too much, for the ways that I neglected myself and ignored my own needs. I was trying to be so "there" for others, to win their approval... that I left myself in the dust. I had no limits for being there for someone who needed me, but I was almost never there for myself. I was so busy trying to make others happy and people-please, that my mind was never quiet enough for me to become aware of my needs and wants. I was focused on others and maintaining low conflict and that took all my energy. There was none left for me and my life. I didn't attend to my own needs. I learned that setting limits and boundaries is truly a sacred self-honoring act that says to me, "I matter. I am worthy of taking back some of the time I spend being there for other people."

Another part of grieving was that with my precious children, I found it easy to be very affectionate and physically there for them. I was easily able to have fun with them. We did all the things like reading books, watching Disney movies, tickling, getting ice cream. However, I had no idea that one thing was missing from my parenting, a very important part - I wasn't able to be there for them, emotionally.

I learned that when we aren't in touch with our own feelings as parents, we certainly aren't capable of being present to another's feelings, and worst of all, to our children's feelings. I couldn't teach them what I didn't know. It was my responsibility to be at my healthiest emotionally and learn what my children needed from me. I grieved deeply as the realization came to light that I wasn't available to them much emotionally because I wasn't able to be emotionally available to me. My children were the one thing I was convinced I was doing well! How could I have missed their emotional needs? I'm sure I didn't miss them 100%, but I knew I'd missed them enough for them to have pain. I had to be aware also that my grieving, although healing, could bring out my perfectionistic, mean-girl, self-beatings. I needed compassion and forgiveness from myself, not another harsh, beat-down of negative self-loathing. I had to accept the reality and grieve it, without allowing my self-talk to take me down a path of guilt and regret. I had to forgive myself and know that I had done the best I could with what I knew.

As Maya Angelou says,

"Do your best, and when you know better, do better."

Acceptance is a big part of grieving. Accepting reality is, in fact, sanity. When I began to accept my past and the things that had shaped me, I no longer had to resist it, deny it, or wonder if I was crazy. My past happened and I was ready to accept it and do whatever I needed to do to be okay, to be happy. Even if everyone around me denied that it happened, denied that it was exactly what it was, I could choose to live in reality. That was part of my grieving, too. Not everyone wanted to acknowledge that there was a problem because they, too, were stuck in denial. A family member might say, "I don't want to hear about your childhood. Deal with it in therapy!" You can't force others to see it if they don't want to, and living in denial is their right. I, however, refuse to deny *what is* because to do that *makes me feel crazy*! Not only that, denial means nothing is going to change and no one is going to grow. Therefore, families stay stuck in these unhealthy generational patterns, causing decades of pain and sadness. I do not want that for my family and future generations. I knew changing myself and my generation would be a BIG project, but I had a burning passion inside driving me—my love for me, my love for my kids and future grandkids, my love for my clients.

So, how did I begin to grieve? I kept showing up early in the morning with my journal, my cup of coffee, and my open and at times, scared heart. I took the thoughts and the sadness that were swirling around in my head and my heart and I put them down on paper. Emptying myself of these feelings left me with so much peace and calm. Eventually, I learned to add meditation - breathing out sadness and breathing in peace and calm and love. (I have developed a deeper self-care course that goes into greater detail about this. The link for this course is at the beginning of this book on page 12, Tools for Your Empowerment.) I began to realize that anxiety and depression were my friends, not my disorder. They were sending a message from my soul saying to me: "Cindy, something has to change--you must stop carrying these racing thoughts. You must sit down and write it down, process it, give it to your higher power, accept it, and then let it go!" After spending time each day, writing and getting the feelings and the sadness out, asking the universe for wisdom and writing that down too, I felt a calm come over me and I began to have strings of good days.

Processing is coming to the realization that your unhealed parents' or caregivers' own wounding's got in the way of you feeling cared for and loved. For example, an unhealed parent may be carrying unprocessed, tremendous anger and yell and scream with an angry face. This manifests in a child's little heart the following: "my parents hate me; I'm so bad and defective that my parents have to act like this; I cause so much trouble for my parents; I must be a burden; I am unlovable." Psychologically, young children are unable to see their parents as bad or defective so when parents treat them badly and react in anger, the child sees himself as bad and that sets up the shame which is the message, "I'm bad" inside the child. Therefore, processing is seeing how your unhealed parents' behaviors affected you and your beliefs about yourself, and realizing, it was never about you. You never had to own those beliefs about yourself that came from your unhealed parents' verbal and emotional carelessness.

Another part of the process I had to learn was to truly love myself. Loving yourself entails something that psychology refers to as re-parenting. With re-parenting, the adult part of you, the part of you that is doing or has done the work in therapy and is reading healthy books, can now become the new loving and kind, "parent voice" inside of you. I like to call this new parent *my higher self*. This is the part of me that is conscious, and has deep compassion, kindness, and a depth of love for me and for all living things. This part of us is the one who will be the re-parent of the little, younger parts, living in our subconscious, who need to be re-cared for and re-nurtured. It sounds strange. You may be thinking, "Cindy, are you saying there are different parts of me inside me? Are you saying I have multiple personality?" No! You do not have multiple personalities. You are not disordered. We all have these different parts. These parts are different aged parts of ourselves who were wounded or didn't receive proper nurturing—one of mine was the protector I wrote about in earlier chapters. Whenever you, as an adult, act like a child (ie. throwing a temper tantrum), that's a little part of you, a younger part, that is wounded and in need of healing.

There's a beautiful freedom that you get to experience when you practice loving these little wounded parts of yourself. You belong to you, so you no longer need external validation that you belong. In other words, when you love yourself, you don't need others' approval to be happy. Healthy others are great to do life with! However, you don't need others' approval or validation that you are okay because with the practice of re-parenting and selflove you begin to believe the universal truth that you are worthy, as are all living beings.

We all carry some pain and fear as our unhealed caregivers were unable to give us the love and nurturing that our little developing brains needed. There simply are no perfect parents. Not getting your needs met as a child does not mean your parents were bad people. It does not mean that you should blame your parents. First of all, that's not helpful. Second, most parents, not all of course, but most, when they have a baby think to themselves, "I love this little cutie, and I want to do my best to be a good parent to this child." I know that's what my parents thought. That's what I thought when I became a parent. We all intend to do our best, but our own unhealed pain gets in the way of doing our best.

The problem with being the best parents we can be comes in because we are still in pain, still very much hurting children ourselves, while trying our best to be an adult parent. Maybe your parents didn't have any guidance or resources to get guidance. I once heard someone say, "There's always a reason behind why one causes pain to another, but never an excuse." Please don't hear me making excuses for emotionally immature parents, or toxic parents. There are some parents that, even though they learn there's a better way, they choose not to own it and get the much needed help. Again, as Maya says, "...once you know better. Do better!" Some people take this seriously; others choose to do nothing. The truth is every parent has a free will and choices to make.

Something that has baffled me as a therapist: I spent seven plus years getting through college, graduate school, and supervision learning how to be a good, best practices, therapist. I spent not one day being educated on how to be a parent before I brought my first child, Matthew, home from the hospital. I remember years ago, I was riding home in my car with my baby in the car seat. He was perfect. He was beautiful. His little eyes were looking to me for answers to questions like: "Who am I?" "Am I enough?" "Do I matter?" "Do you love me?" The answer to all of those questions for my son, of course, was a resounding, "Yes!" That is the answer to all of those questions for all children. Was I able to convey that to mine? Maybe some. But because I was so wounded myself, I was only able to give to them as much as I believed that for myself. Parents can only give their children the emotional security that they have created for themselves. If you don't have something, you certainly can't pass it to someone else. If I didn't believe those things for me, how was I going to help my children believe it? This is why it is critical for people, especially parents to DO THEIR WORK. I believe as a society, we could do better at some type of psycho-education for new parents. Once I realized my own parenting needed help, I reached out for the only thing I had to help me: parenting books and therapy - things that are not available to everyone.

The hurt parts of us are like little kids sometimes: boundaryless and out of control. When you have reacted to something at a level "10" that was worthy of only a level "2" response, did you think, "Why did I react so intensely? Why did that affect my reaction so much? What's wrong with me? Do I have an anger problem?" You realize you were out of line. That level "10" reaction is telling you that you have unhealed wounds. It's called "being triggered." For example, your child does something careless that all children do, like slam the door, and you shoot up from your chair and yell at them. That's your own wound, or fear, being "triggered" and show-ing up in a completely unrelated situation. This was a signal to me, as a parent, that I needed help. Something was unhealed inside me and I needed to explore what it was before I hurt my own children. My unhealed trauma, my level "10" reactions, my fear, my anger, my resentment and my anxiety were all begging me to ask for help for myself.

Everyone gets to make the choice either to *do the work* or not; to seek help from a therapist or not. Most of us choose to close our eyes and chase the tyranny of the urgent, whether that is busyness, denial, addiction to food, alcohol, shopping, or drugs. Whatever dependence of choice that allows you to ignore the pain inside yourself is what most of us choose, mostly out of our conditioning or subconscious. Therefore, when I wasn't doing my healing work, I was continuing to pass my pain to those around me. When I was ignoring my own pain, I couldn't take responsi-bility for it. I couldn't humbly apologize. I couldn't own what I did to hurt another.

I know there are other theories regarding addiction. Many people believe that addiction is a disease and people who are addicted are victims of the disease. In some cases that may be true. However, I also believe addiction can be an escape or a way we make for ourselves to avoid or deny our woundings and our emotions. I believe the disease theory may be true in some cases, not because I want to place blame on anyone. It's quite the opposite. I dislike theories that make people perpetual victims. A victim stance renders one powerless. I am a social worker. One of my highest values is that everyone has the ability to tap into his or her own personal strengths and use that personal power over their problems. I'll not dive deep into this debate because it is beyond the scope of this book.

The people hurt by our avoidance and denial of feelings are not only ourselves, but are our children. You wouldn't believe the power a parent has in owning his/her part and apologizing. There is power in having a conversation with your children and inviting them to share how they felt when you were out of control. You can validate their feelings, and *own all of it*. It's a healing salve on a heart with an open, gaping wound. This is one of the most profound healers of relationships: owning and apologizing. It brings healing for both parties, the pain giver and the pain receiver. But this takes humility and radical ownership.

In the past when I worked with teens, I invited parents of my teen clients to my office when it became clear to me, after talking to the young client, that she was in pain because of the way her wounded parents were wounding her. It was interesting how this was the case almost every time I had a teen client who was in trouble or even suicidal. With my teen client's full approval, I would sit with the parents and explain, "Your daughter is in pain. The reason she is harming herself, cutting into her body with a knife, is because the pain is overwhelming. You, as her parents, can be part of the healing if you choose. She desperately wants a relationship with you, she wants to be seen and heard by you, and she desperately needs some of your time. She needs to hear from you that, apart from all of your expectations of her, she is loved unconditionally. Your daughter is suicidal. If you are willing to work with me, I can teach you how to be there for her, how to navigate and improve your relationship with her." You wouldn't believe how many parents look at me with eyes rolled, and say,

"She has it ten times better than we did! We've given that girl everything - the best schools, the best neighborhood. Everything she could ever ask for." I have to breathe and realize these parents can't hear me. They don't get what I'm telling them at all. They are not ready. All they can focus on is their own pain. They can't have compassion for their daughter because of their own unhealed wounds. They walk out of my office the same way they walked in. Nothing changes. They did what so many generations have done and continue to do: sweep the generational pain under the rug. It's so very sad.. But, it's the truth and it's the result of unhealed pain that runs through generations of families until someone says "this hurtful, painful abuse is ending with me!" These heroes get help, do the hard work, heal, and begin to change the generational patterns within their generation. And they own the parenting that went awry before the work was done.

Simply because we may consider our child's pain less than what we endured as a child, does not mean it's not pain. Simply because we believe our children have it better than we did, doesn't mean we don't have a responsibility to do our own healing and stop perpetuating pain on our children. Someone once said, "hurt people, hurt people." It's that simple. None of us gets to measure someone else's pain. Plain and simple.

I continued seeing my therapist until I felt I'd grieved most of my pain, until I felt I had no more tears to cry. After my grieving season came another life reorganization. After I grieved all of what I was dealing with in my loneliness, I could begin to find my tribe. Grieving and finding new people are ongoing processes. New grief will come up from time to time, but I recognize what it is and allow the feeling to come to the surface and feel it as needed. I began asking and praying for healthy friends who had been in some process of healing their own lives. Slowly, people began to come into my life, friends with whom I could have coffee and talk about ideas and life. Eleanor Roosevelt said, "Great minds discuss ideas, average minds discuss events, small minds discuss people." I was looking for friends who talked about ideas and events, life goals, and a determination to live as their higher selves.

I was done with talking about other people, with being judgmental; with trying to make myself feel better by tearing someone else down and with playing the comparison game. I was done! No one is perfect. I still do my fair share of messing up. The difference is that today I will own it and apologize when I realize I've made a mess. I've had clients ask me, "Do people ever arrive? Will I ever get so enlightened that I arrive?" I believe we can become enlightened with knowledge and peace and new behaviors, but I don't believe we arrive at a place where we no longer need check-ins with a mirror. We're human and as long as we are alive I believe we can continue learning and growing. I'm sure I will be learning and growing until I take my last breath. I want to be more and more like the loving Spirit of the Universe, of course. That's my goal. I think, rather than arrive. We work on ourselves and become heroes who stop trying to save others and instead, save our own selves! We begin to live our lives from our higher selves. Not all heroes wear capes. Sometimes they are ordinary people who wanted change, did the work and now pay it forward by helping.

JOURNAL PROMPTS

- Do you have some grieving to do regarding your past?
- Are their parts of you that you want to forgive yourself for not knowing what you didn't know?
- Where are you still beating yourself up?
- How can you grow and heal in order to change your future generations? (Do you want to be a hero?)
- If you are a parent, are there some things you could own and apologize to your kids for? Is there some personal work you need to do to be the parent you can be?

Chapter 7

Realize That You Have a Purpose
(and it's never too late)!

I walked through the university doors. The smell of books was familiar and reminded me of my high school days a couple of decades ago. I waited in the Student Center line for a few minutes, reading the posts on the walls and checking out the other students. They were much younger. Actually, they were close to my own children's ages, as I had two in high school and one in middle school. Finally, it was my turn in line. The lady sized me up with her eyes and said, "How can I help you?" My voice cracked, "I want to sign up for the next semester and I'd like to find out how to do that."

I was 37 years old and facing two mountains: a bachelor's and a master's degree. I was standing at the bottom of "Bachelor Degree Mountain," asking what gear I would need to scale it. I was determined to have a career that I would absolutely love, that I would be passionate about and that would have the purpose of serving others. I could see the writing on the wall at home - change was coming.

My children were growing up and leaving home in the next few years. My career as a domestic engineer, or stay-at-home mom for the past 18 years, was coming to an end. And I was sad. When your kids are little, you think they will be home forever. Even though you know that's not true, somehow it feels like they will be underfoot, in your home, always. You know you're preparing them to leave as they grow older, but it feels like that day won't really ever come. Maybe it's the hope it won't come. It was a weird feeling, and I've talked to several women who have felt the same kind of emptiness around raising independent children who leave. I kind of think being a woman/mother can be a really emotionally difficult thing, because your life changes a lot. For example, you have babies, then toddlers, then preteens, then teenagers (big eye roll there LOL), then college, then your kids get married, then new in-law kids come into the family, and then grandchildren… forever changing. New adjustments, new acceptances, new ways of relating to your children as they grow and become adults…. all of it was, for me, A LOT! I saw this train of my kids becoming independent coming down the tracks, and I wanted to make sure I didn't try to hold them back like I wanted to (when you grow up in fear, you tend to want to CONTROL). I recognized this about myself… that I needed to create a life of my own now that my "mom career" was coming to a close.

Ever since the time I entered therapy at around age 29, I started dreaming about becoming a therapist. I love people. I also love quiet, beautiful offices, and I wanted to help people in the ways I had been helped. It always seemed like a far-fetched dream for me because I didn't have a great deal of confidence. I had not accomplished much that the world would acknowledge. College seemed like a huge under-taking for someone like me. I didn't really apply myself in high school because I was geared more toward the social aspects. I loved planning for the weekends and hanging out with my friends , mostly. Academics were more of a necessary evil. But, one day I declared, "I'm doing this! I will be okay as the oldest student in those college classes! I will be okay with school loans! I'm putting myself on the front line for once. It's time for me to do me!" I was throwing off that people-pleaser cape that had been holding me back and pulling me down and I putting myself on top of my list!

I arrived home that night, after meeting with the college advisor, signing up for my first semester, and taking a tour of the campus. Suddenly, it hit me. The gremlins came in full force at that moment and I thought, "What are you doing? You can't do this! Who do you think you are?" I found myself on my bed in the fetal position, full of regret at signing up for college.

This is what I used to face whenever I had a huge decision before me: the gremlins, the conditioning voices of the past! I think most of us have gremlins, or doubts, about our place in the world. I think most of us stop here, though, and never accomplish what we dream about. I was about to quit before I started. I think most of us allow the gremlins to have the last say in our lives.

I had done that to myself for too long. I refused to let fear take me down. Fear is a real issue when we try to do something that seems out of our reach. The fear was from my conditioning and I knew it. So I took a breath, and tried to become more present. We can either let fear and the gremlins win, or we can try to be conscious and keep walking toward our dreams of who we are meant to be and what we are meant to do—scared to death!

I hear clients in their 30's and 40's say all the time, "I'm stuck in this job that I hate. I'm too old to do something different. I'm too old to go back to school. I'm too old to pursue what I really want to pursue. I'm too old to follow my dream of what I believe I was put on the planet to do." These are fear statements of your childhood conditioning. These are not the truth. These are the gremlins going out of control inside our heads. You're only too old to do something you want to do when you're dead, and not a minute before! There was an 80-something year old woman in some of my classes. She was rocking it. I remember saying to myself, when I started my journey in college, "You will be 42 years old when you finish graduate school. You will arrive at age 42 no matter what and one of two things can be true: you will turn 42 and have no degrees, or you will turn 42 and be finishing up your master's degree. Will it be hard? Maybe. Will people think you are wasting time and money? Perhaps. Nobody wants to have school debt at age 42." I decided I wanted to be 42 and finishing up school so that I could do what I had been dreaming about doing for ten years. It's never too late to change your life. If I can do it, anyone can.

What have you been dreaming of doing? Go for it with all you've got! The argument that it's a financially ignorant decision to switch gears in mid-life is just that, an argument. My husband and I developed a mantra early on in our marriage/family: People trump money! Your fulfillment is more valuable than money. I once heard someone say,

> *"We go to pre-school to prepare for grade school; we go to grade school to prepare for middle school; we go to middle school to prepare for high school; we go to high school to prepare for college; we go to college to prepare for our career; we work for 40+ years to prepare for retirement."*

We're always preparing for something else, something in the future, and rarely actually living our present lives to the fullest. None of us can predict how long we will be on the planet, so why not for the time you do have here do something you will love waking up for in the morning?

Oscar Wilde said,

"To live is the rarest thing in the world. Most people just exist."

Don't settle for existence and Groundhog Days. Make sure whatever you do that each day is something you love. Not everyone has to go to school to do what they love. There are many ways to do what you love. My point is, you matter - and what you love matters enough for you to do what needs to be done to make it happen.

Who are you? Do you know?

I didn't know who I was for many years. I basically thought my identity was in my roles: daughter, mom, wife, friend. That's not who I was. Who was I? It took me looking into the pain of my past catapulting me into therapy, to figure it out. While in therapy, I learned that I was a real, feeling, unique person. I was me. I was not my roles. My roles were not what made me, me. They didn't define me as a person. I am me. I am an ambivert. I love being with people and, after a while, I have to get away from all people to be alone and recharge. I am creative. I love art, writing, decorating. I am spiritual. Since I was a little girl, I have had big questions about where I come from. Is there a God? Who is God? I am also, funny. I love to make people laugh. I love to laugh. I am smart. I love to learn new things. I am, uniquely, me.

Before learning who I was, my interests were other people. I looked outside of me to others. What did others feel? What were others' opinions? What did they wear? How did they decorate? I looked at others and was so amazed that they knew what their opinions were, they knew what they wanted to do with their lives, they knew what things they stood for and they knew with what things they didn't care to be bothered. I knew none of this for myself. Not really. I was mostly copying other's opinions, beliefs, and ways. I was what is called a codependent.

I began to spend time alone, journaling my thoughts, listening to my knowing, getting to know me. It was a very interesting journey. These are some of my bravest accomplishments. Feeling your feelings is not for the faint of heart. It's for the brave. It requires vulnerability, letting your guard down, trusting someone else, trusting yourself, trusting the process. It was not easy. It was hard. The payoff is peace and freedom. I shared earlier in the chapter that I went to get my bachelor's degree and my master's degree at the age of thirty-seven. I finally was beginning the journey to know me. It was not too late. I wake up most days feeling excited to do my life and be in my life! You can't buy this! You can't manufacture this! You can only do it one step at a time, starting wherever you are right now.

It hasn't been easy. I admit that. I wondered, "What would people think if I shared my story? Maybe I should keep this a secret. I will wear make-up, the right clothes, hair, and will keep my past a secret." I remember when I had my babies, thinking, "They will never know. They won't ever know my pain. I will protect them from pain." We all know how delusional that is. I carried these secrets for years, until I no longer could. Being honest about me and my past actually turned out to be a surprise gift. Being a therapist and having those past experiences only helped my clients. I wasn't an educated talking head… I was a real person with real past pain, now healed.

Sometimes, I think we get the idea that we can only help people if we have it all together, and actually the very opposite is true! What you've been through in your life and what you *heal from* is the secret sauce that helps others have the courage to heal!

When I listened to my heart that morning on that retreat I wrote about in Utah, I decided to take my personal power back. I began to desire that the things that happened to me over the years would somehow, in some way, have value to me and to others. Was there some way I could take the horror of my past and turn it into something redeeming, something beautiful, like the kintsugi bowl art? Could I possibly see it as a gift to be used to help other women? The answer was YES!

The Legend of *Kintsugi*

A Japanese legend tells the story of a mighty shogun warrior who broke his favorite tea bowl and sent it away for repairs. When he received it back, the bowl was held together by unsightly metal staples. Although he could still use it, the shogun was disappointed. Still hoping to restore his beloved bowl to its former beauty, he asked a craftsman to find a more elegant solution.

The craftsman wanted to try a new technique, something that would add to the beauty of the bowl as well as repair it. So, he mended every crack in the bowl with a lacquer resin mixed with gold. When the tea bowl was returned to the shogun, there were streaks of gold running through it, telling its story, and—the warrior thought—adding to its value and beauty. This method of repair became known as kintsugi.

Kintsugi, which roughly translates to "golden joinery," is the Japanese philosophy that the value of an object is not in its beauty, but in its imperfections, and that these imperfections are something to celebrate, not hide.

(from: Youniquefoundation.org)

We are so beautiful in our imperfections, and in our brokenness. We aren't broken beyond repair when we have past pain. We, like the kintsugi art bowl, become masterpieces as we do our work of healing. Our healing journey is like the gold that puts our lives back together. Because by being healed, we are more valuable to ourselves and other people with whom we may inspire.

I was no longer feeling like the shamed, worthless girl anymore. I'll never forget the words of my therapist when she said, "The abuse was not your fault! It was never your fault!" So many who are abused say they feel they were at fault in some way. It feels that way but it's simply not true. The dark cloud I'd carried over my head for most of my life was beginning to dissolve. I realized that the shame wasn't mine to carry. I wanted the pain to mean something, to help someone else who was suffering, to be of service somehow. I know there are millions of other women who find themselves in the pit of shame, feeling used, attributing the abuse to themselves, to who they are, as if they deserved it.

I learned that day in the mountains, that I didn't deserve that. No one deserves that. Everyone has pain, and those who have been abused, or assaulted in any way certainly don't deserve to be shamed. I refused to allow my own abuse and shame to have the last word in my life. I wanted more than anything to no longer refer to myself as wounded, but rather to refer to myself as a wounded healer. I was no longer a broken bowl in pieces, but a bowl, beautiful and pieced back together with gold. It had to be real. I had to be real. Wounded healers aren't anything if they are not real, if they are not authentic. It had to be something I felt and knew in my heart, not something I only believed in my mind.

"Nobody escapes being wounded. We are all wounded people, whether physically, emotionally, mentally, or spiritually. The main question is not, 'How can we hide our wounds?' so that we don't have to be embarrassed, but 'How can we put our woundedness in the service of others?' When our wounds cease to be a source of shame, and become a source of healing, we have become wounded healers." ~Henry Nouwen

Many clients say, "I don't even want to share the things that have happened to me!"

"It's so embarrassing."

"You're the only person I've ever shared this story with." "No one knows my true story, but you."

"I've kept it inside, until now." "It's like I wear a scarlet letter!"

We women carry so much shame around, shame that someone else perpetuated on us. Why? Why do we take it and not say anything? I was watching the Jeffrey Epstein Documentaries and could identify with the girls and women who said, "It just happened. I was there and he was touching me, and I didn't know what to do.'" It's as if we would be bothering somebody: "Excuse me, I hate to bother you, but I've been violently assaulted and I'm sorry to say those strong words and I hope you're not put off." Ridiculous! But that truly is how I felt for a long time. I know some of you feel that way, too. It makes me very sad and very concerned. When will we teach our girls, with our actions, that we are worthy as women; that we are enough; that we matter enough to say, "Get off of me!" and then run, not walk, to tell everyone what happened to us? We will do this when we no longer feel shame and blame for what another human being decided to do to us without our permission, no matter what we were wearing. It took me so long to share it because I needed to realize this was not my fault.

I can't express the honor and responsibility I feel when a client shares her deepest, heart-held secrets and darkest feelings with me. I feel like I'm being given a precious stone, and I feel like whispering as though something holy just happened. It's because something holy did just happen. A woman felt worthy enough to share her pain and her abuse. I believe vulnerability and sharing your deepest secrets and pain is very holy and spiritual, as well as life giving. Healing is a second chance at life; a second chance at being able to love yourself like the Divine loves you; a second chance to pursue your dreams. It is such a great privilege to do this work. We don't have to be embarrassed at someone else's poor choice to hurt us. We don't have to continue the cycle of taking responsibility for an abuser's choices. The only responsibility we have in our abuse is to get our beautiful, amazing selves the help we need to heal.

Once I felt whole again, mostly healed of my past, I wanted to shout from the mountaintop: "It's possible! It's completely possible to feel good again; to not feel at fault, in shame, and worthless everyday deep inside! It's not only possible but it's amazing!" That's the message for anyone who reads this. You can heal. You can feel as good as new again! If I can, you can, any woman can. You can wake up and feel happy to be alive! I'm proof. I want to be in service to helping others heal.

What are you passionate about? What do you love? What would make you wake up every morning and say, "I can't wait to go to work today?" Do whatever you can to make it happen. Will it be awkward at times? Yes, and sometimes it will be difficult. It's your life. It's that valuable. You have gifts to share. Make it a priority to share them!

JOURNAL PROMPTS

- Do you see the value in healing your past?
- What steps will you take toward getting help with healing?
- Is there something you've secretly been dreaming about becoming or doing?
- What gifts do you have that you have been hiding?

Chapter 8

Every Woman Needs
a Spiritual Practice

I talk with women every day in my coaching practice who are educated, smart, talented, capable, "kicking-ass-in-their-careers" kind of women. However, when it comes to their personal lives, the words "shit show" comes up. Women that could run an army of employees come home and it's as if they allow tanks to roll over them while they lay on the floor.

These women, in most areas, are bright, intuitive and sexy; and yet at home, they feel stupid, incapable, confused, and unable to figure out why they go through relationship after relationship where they are treated badly, taken advantage of, manipulated to feel that they are always the problem and made to feel responsible for fixing another's mess. They date men that don't treat them like they deserve. Their children run over the top of them. Their children are out of control. These women set good boundaries in their business dealings while, at home, they resemble guilty, soggy marshmallows. This was me, too, before creating a daily spiritual practice. The daily practice is key to self-awareness! Self-awareness is the catalyst for knowing what you want and getting what you want out of life!

Women are incredibly nurturing creatures by nature and most of us generally don't enjoy disappointing people. Therefore, many of us say "yes" when we mean "no." We close our eyes and say to ourselves, with our fists clinched under the table, "I can do this. I can take that on. I can handle that," especially with our kids. And not far behind, in creeps resentment and guilt. Over and over, we acquiesce to the needs of those around us and put our own needs and wants up on a shelf, with the intention of getting to them later.

Eventually, we find we've lost ourselves and have no idea who we are or what we want anymore. We realize that we have become a somewhat invisible person somewhere along the way and have no idea where to begin to find ourselves. We ask, "Who am I? How did I get here?" Then we begin to beat ourselves up for losing ourselves. We shame ourselves with, "What is wrong with me?"

Here's the good news - nothing is wrong with you! You have a great, big, beautiful heart and too much love for everyone on the entire planet, *except for yourself.* One day, we recognize and admit that we have placed ourselves on the shelf, dusty and crusty.

The point here is, you matter. You are not a victim of the people who always take advantage of you. *You* are sometimes the one taking advantage of you. You are loving everyone so well - everyone but *you.* An exhausted client of mine asked, "When does the shit end?" I said, "It ends when WE say it does and start prioritizing ourselves and setting boundaries with ourselves."

When I began to prioritize myself, I had to find a block of time in each and every day to spend with ME—I called it "quiet time," or "my daily spiritual practice," "alone time," whatever. I choose to spend this block of time, at the same time early each morning to read, meditate, journal, pray, or just sit with myself. I hope I can convey to you the miracle that this practice brings to my life. When I say "miracle," I mean that if I do this one thing each day, I am more present in my day, my life, and to those I love and care for. It's miraculous! I say that because when I didn't set this practice time aside for myself, I felt hurried, crabby, tired, and on edge. Miraculous in that I have 1-2 hours a day less time (because that's the time I spend with me), and yet I am more present for me and for others. I actual have less time in my day but it feels as though I have more t.i.m.e., because I'm present and nurtured. Does that make sense?

Another miracle of my daily spiritual practice is that I feel less guilt, less resentment, more happy and more loving. It's been quite an amazing experience. We aren't robots. We have bodies, so we give them time, most days, to workout. We also have souls, hearts, and minds. Those deserve at least as much time per day as we spend working out for our bodies, don't you think?

One day I was sitting in my comfy chair with my pumpkin coffee, typical for my daily spiritual practice. I was pondering something I'd read: "We cannot love anyone well, not our kids, no one, until we learn to love ourselves well." I was thinking, "What? Love ourselves? Is that even a thing really? Doesn't that mean I'll be selfish and conceited, maybe even become narcissistic?" Then I thought, "This is nonsense! It has to be because I love my husband, I love every one of my children, I love my family and my friends *more than anything*!" There it is: *more than anything*. I love them more than I love me! Is it possible to know how others need to be loved before we know what *we* need to be and feel loved? In exploring this for some time, I have concluded that the answer is, "No!"

We must experience the journey, the acts of truly loving ourselves, which requires acceptance of our bodies, our short-comings, warts and all. Only then, are we capable of truly, genuinely loving others. So, what is this thing we've been doing for everybody else, thinking we're loving them well? Probably, if I'm honest, deep down, my self-esteem and confidence were not where they needed to be for me to be whole. I was people-pleasing, and I was unknowingly trying to win other's love, other's approval. That's not real self-love.

My lack of love for myself and low self-esteem, modeled "love" as denying oneself and laying down one's life to take care of others. I also enabled bad behavior. I did for others what others were perfectly capable of doing for themselves—in other words, ENABLING—(speaking mostly to moms here - did you know that if we do too much for our kids, it actually sets them back in life? Now that mine are all grown, I get wisdom all the time about the things I did or didn't do and how it affected my kids good or bad). Sometimes, making other people happy by doing things for *them*, ends up disappointing *us*. Most times, you will disappoint someone. If you choose to not disappoint you, others will be disappointed. If you choose others, it's you who's disappointed.

We are responsible for ourselves, ultimately. Of course, it goes without saying, but I'll say it here, there are exceptions: young children, disabled people, the mentally challenged. We must, at times, first take care of those in our care who cannot take care of themselves. I want to make that clear. But even there, we can enable people to be less than they could possibly be by getting in there and doing for them that which they can do to take care of themselves.

Survivors of dysfunctional family dynamics were made to feel as children that they didn't matter enough to be seen or heard; that their feelings didn't count; that they weren't important to the family, and that only the parents' feelings mattered. That's a lie that needs to be set on fire in our own hearts and minds. That is the one thing that if we don't heal it - if we don't change it - we will never live our own lives to the fullest. You matter.

I know what it's like to wake up day after day taking care of other people while ignoring my own life and myself. I got very lost. I'm going to tell you something that is not easy for me to admit. It may sound a little weird, but it is my experience. There were a couple of years of my life in my 30's where I heard, not audibly, but I sensed a question go through my mind several times a day. The question was, "Do you want to marry me?" After a while of hearing it, it really began to bother me for two reasons. The first reason was it didn't make sense. The second reason was I didn't know where it was coming from. At the time this was happening to me, I was married, mostly happily, for some years. I thought, "Where is this coming from? Who is saying this to me? Is this God? If it is, what is Spirit trying to tell me? I'm already married." I even remember thinking, "Is this God trying to tell me I'm not in the right marriage?" Day after day, month after month, I would hear, "Do you want to marry me?" This was so perplexing for me, as you can imagine.

It wasn't until a few years later that the meaning of that question resonated with me. I was sitting in my living room, one early morning, during my practice/quiet time. The knowing came to me that it was my soul who was asking me this question. Why would my soul be asking me to marry it? I'll explain.

For example, in my marriage to Steve, I am loyal to him. I love him deeply. I went wherever I needed to go so that he could pursue what he saw as his "calling." I moved to Kentucky so that he could pursue a graduate degree; and then to Texas so that he could finish graduate school. I moved back to Ohio so that he could pursue his dream of creating a non-profit startup. I love him. I helped him make tough decisions. We would talk for hours about everything. I made him his favorite dinners. I cleaned our house and decorated it beautifully. I had sex 3.5x a week. I made his home beautiful. I did many things to create a beautiful and meaningful life for him. I raised our three children while he was at school, and work, and meetings. I was there! I was his right-hand woman. I had his back. I worked hard so his life would be easier, more beautiful, less complicated. I was on a mission to love him the best I knew how.

So, I thought, "I guess that's what my soul wants of me." But part of me also wanted to be married to, or in a deeper relationship with, me. My soul wanted me to love myself with the same passion with which I loved Steve. I realize how weird this sounds, but stay with me. My focus in my marriage was Steve. I'd watched my grandmothers' focus be my grandfathers. I'd witnessed my mom's focus be my dad. I watched my mom on some days clean from morning until late afternoon, make dinner, and then, I'd watch her brush her hair and put makeup on for my dad's arrival home from work. As best I knew, this was my job. I lost myself being married to Steve. I thought this was the "Christian way," "a good wife's duties," "the ways of a woman." This is what my family and church taught me - my conditioning.

Steve didn't ask me to do any of these things for him. He wasn't responsible for me being obsessed with making his life great. He didn't demand I do this. He's a very easy-going type of person. He never complained if he came home to a messy house, no dinner, kids and toys everywhere or me on the couch in a heap. When Steve came in from work on a day like this, he would check on me, play with the kids, order pizza and pick up toys. He never said anything like, "Look, woman, this is your job to make me happy!" Never. But, in my mind, it was my job. I didn't even think about what I wanted. Maybe once every six years I'd say, "I want a new couch." Some days, I may want a cute new top. Or on some Friday nights, I'd want to order carry-out for dinner. Other than that, there was nothing I wanted. I was content. I was happy.

However, I wasn't *really* content or happy. One day, sitting on my couch, I was thinking about Steve. This dark cloud came over me as I was in my resentment, and I thought about how great his life was with me in it. I thought about "all I do for that man!" He came home from work one day and I glared at him and said, "Just who do you think you are?" In other words, "Who do you think you are to live your life the way you want it, be gone all the time and leave me here to do all the work? Who do you think you are to go to graduate school while I'm cooking and cleaning and raising our three kids? Must be nice!" I sneered. I looked at Steve and he looked back at me like a deer in headlights. This went on for a few minutes. Then, he asked, "What happened, Cindy? Where is this coming from? Cindy, you know you can do whatever you want. I will support anything you want, honey! What do you want? Do you want to go to school?" He gave me that blank look men sometimes give, as if they have just been made to drink out of a firehose and we ask them, "Why are you all wet?"

It was then I realized that I had wrongly placed the blame. I needed to take responsibility for how I spent my time. I never once asked myself, "Cindy, what do you love? What are you passionate about? What is it that makes you stay up late and think for hours? What makes you get really excited? What do you want to do? What do you want to be good at besides your roles of wife and mom?" I had begun to realize that I was the one totally ignoring myself and my needs, not him. I was not a victim of Steve. I was a victim of my own doing. I had to take personal responsibility for my own life and happiness. No one can do that for me. Now, one part of me was asking another part of me to marry me, basically, asking *me* to love *me* as much as I loved Steve and to take care of myself the way I took care of Steve.

Is it possible to love yourself like that? Do people really love themselves? Isn't that selfish? Isn't that conceited? Do people have compassion for themselves? Wouldn't that make me a weak, whiney person? Do people give themselves grace like they give it to others? Wouldn't that mean I'm not taking personal responsibility? I had all kinds of thoughts and questions from my childhood conditioning swirling through my mind.

I had to decide whether or not anyone was on board. I had to make a vow to love myself first. I had to become whole. I had to learn how to love myself. I had to make it possible for me to become the person I was put on the planet to be. I had to become someone I could admire! I did not want to be someone else's idea of who I was supposed to be. I did not want to be my mother's idea or my grandmothers' idea of who I should be. I wanted to be fully me. Maybe I would choose to work at home, raising my children. The key word here is "choose." Choose it, not because my mom did it, not because her mother did it, but choose it for me. I had to make a vow to myself. I had to begin to love myself if I was going to become a whole person.

It's a requirement. It's also an option. But to not love ourselves would mean quieting (killing) our hearts and souls and doing what we don't want to do. Up would spring bitterness and resentment, the possibility of disease from it all and sometimes, death.

How do we begin to love ourself daily? We begin by prioritizing ourselves and creating a spiritual practice. This had to begin inside me. I had to know that I mattered, and my life was important enough to me to spend at least an hour a day alone with myself (the hour is not the point - you may pick another amount of time for you). This is where I evaluated my relationships, my time, my joy (or lack of), my goals and dreams. Sometimes all this guilt or resentment we feel isn't even ours to feel... sometimes it's just our society's ideas, but if I don't spend time thinking about it or evaluating, I may just default to guilt and hurried-ness, and misery. We have an opportunity to plan our own lives and how we want them to be. I started at the end of my life in my thinking, wondering "In my last hours, what do I think I'll wish I'd done more of? Laundry? Running to games every night? Watching TV?" Duh, no. What will you wish you'd done more of? More time in relationships? More time working on your dream? Starting a business? Volunteering? Whatever those answers are for you, FIND THEM... take the time to find out. You matter.

One of the first places I had to start evaluating was my voice. I had to commit to begin speaking up for myself. I'd almost never spoken up for myself. If someone would say something about me, to me, that was negative, I automatically sunk back in shame and either believed it or spent a great amount of time ruminating over it, like a victim. I needed to stop, get quiet with myself and process whether or not I was going to take that advice. Was it from God? Was it what I believed? My opinion matters in the equation now.

Today, I will only listen to loving feedback from people I trust and respect. I will listen and I will form my own understanding of it. I then will return to have another conversation with them, once I've processed it and formed how I want to respond. Any feedback that comes to me with venom, or feels toxic, I don't bother with it. I say to myself, "Consider the source!" and walk away.

My own opinion was squashed early on in my life and through the years from little criticisms I heard and took personally. What we believe about ourselves becomes truth for us, regardless of whether or not it's a lie. I talk to women every single day who were made to feel small, be quiet and be nice. So I know I'm not alone here.

Another way that I found I could work on me in my practice was to help myself have more confidence. This required working on my inner self-talk during my practice. This led to letting go of toxic relationships and honoring myself by having integrity. In the relationships that I considered to be important to me, I came up with better ways for me to relate to them. They didn't have to do anything. Remember, we can only control our own behavior and no one else's. If they had toxic tendencies but I loved them, I would not share my deepest, most vulnerable thoughts. I could love them and be kind and have some conversation, mostly about surface things. I could choose to still have some kind of relationship with them. However, it wasn't a very close relationship. I just didn't want to abandon the relationship altogether. Some people decide to go no contact with some people, and that's a good idea too, in some cases.

As for my vulnerable thoughts - I would save those for the friends who are doing their work and getting healthy; for the people I trusted and knew for sure that they truly want the highest good for me. Those people are my people and they are the only people privy to my most intimate thoughts.

My spiritual practice always comes back to these questions: "What do I want? Where do I feel safe and good and healthy?" These are always the questions I ask and answer for myself when I have the question, "What do I do next?" I get grounded by deep breathing for 10-minutes, getting into and feeling into my body. And if I'm with someone and my body feels nauseous or stiff or if I'm not comfortable or something is off, I don't share my heart. I keep it on the surface. If my body feels comfortable, safe and good, I realize this is a safe person and I can share my heart. It took me a while to be able to feel into my body and ultimately, my intuition. It took years because for most of my childhood, my body was one of the places that was hurt. Therefore, I was disengaged from my body. It was scary for me to think about getting back into my body and feeling my feelings again. However, as I did get back into feeling into my body, she became my holy grail. She never lies. She's wise, knows things and is intuitive.

Another vow I made to me was that I will no longer betray myself. I decided that I needed to decide never to say "yes" when I clearly felt a "no." I would not agree to something that didn't feel right just to please the person asking. I had to matter to me. For the first time, what I felt and wanted and needed was going to be important.

I was always the master of my own life, I just didn't realize it. Like Dorothy in the *Wizard of Oz,* she always had the power. If she could tap the ruby slippers, she would immediately be home, but she just didn't realize it. I had been a terrible master of my life up until now. It was time to learn how to manage my life in which I was the main character because I am ultimately only responsible for myself. This only became reality when I began to spend time with myself in my daily practice.

My son-in-law, Michael, was holding his daughter, my new baby granddaughter, Olivia, when she was about a month old. We were both admiring her, smelling her and basking in the wonder of this new little love who came into our lives. I said to Michael, "Isn't it just so amazing and hard to grasp how much we love this little girl that we don't even really know yet?" She was born and instantly, we all loved her with all our hearts and would lay on railroad tracks for her, no questions asked. He looked me in the eyes, and said, "It's spiritual." Yes! That's what it feels like! And when I vow to love and take care of myself from here on out, practicing a daily ritual, it is spiritual.

In my daily ritual or quiet time, I ask myself, "What is my intention?" When I lived without an "intention," I seemed to live aimlessly which made me feel empty. That's the Groundhog Day thing I was referring to earlier. I talk to women every day in my practice that feel like this: work, eat, sleep, repeat... work, eat, sleep, repeat... Groundhog Day living. No matter what you do on a given day, your life can have purpose and intention. Whether you are a stay-at-home mom, work outside the home in a job or career, it doesn't matter. You can live life on purpose with your own intention. As the seasons of my life were constantly in flux, I had to prepare for myself to handle those changes with grace, as well as not allow myself to be trampled in the process.

I was a stay-at-home mom for 18 years, and I realize how fortunate I am that it was possible. We made a lot of choices for that to be possible. For example, we didn't live in a big, new home. We lived in an older, smaller home. We drove our cars until they wouldn't run anymore. That was my choice. I decided my purpose was to teach my kids, feed them healthily, and create a happy family homelife. This took a great deal of time and intentional planning. I felt I had purpose.

Once my kids were mostly raised and in high school, I could see that creating a home was becoming less time-consuming because my kids were in school, in sports, or working. They weren't home as much in these years. I was bored. I could see the writing on the wall that my time as a mom was heading for a huge change. I wasn't going to be needed in this capacity forever. That's when I decided to go to school and create a career for me.

Now, my kids are adults and living their own lives. My purpose is mostly living my best life, and my private practice. My relationships with my husband, my adult kids and my grandbabies are also very important to my purpose. All of these things are part of what makes a balanced life for me.

Another part of my practice is a daily ritual or check-in with myself. I have a certain chair, with a lamp nearby, coffee, and a basket with a journal, my books, etc. It's like an appointment with myself and my higher power. I process feelings, sometimes in my journal, sometimes just there in that chair. I read helpful books. I ask questions of the Spirit or God, and write answers I seem to get that are encouraging. If you've never asked, try it. If it's encouraging and loving—then you know it's from God. If it's not, it may be your old conditioning coming up and maybe you want to unpack that with a therapist. I set my goals and make my plans. Everyone's daily ritual will look different and that's okay! The point is getting alone with yourself and developing a friendship with you, setting aside time for you, and making yourself a priority. Making space, free space in your calendar for yourself, is so empowering! You deserve it. You matter!

JOURNAL PROMPTS

- What is your relationship with yourself like? Are you happy with it? Could you maybe need to make yourself part of your own priority?

- What is your purpose?

- Do you have a daily ritual, or quiet time with yourself to process, and ask questions? If not, would you like to start one now?

- Where are you putting others who can take care of themselves, ahead of yourself these days?

END NOTES

Chapter 1: See your Worth, Know That you Matter

1. "love your neighbor as yourself " (Mark 12:31 NIV)

Chapter 2: Everyone Can Heal, Even you!

1. **Artist:** RACHEL PLATTEN **Song:** FIGHT SONG Licensed to YouTube by:
LatinAutor - SonyATV, SOLAR Music Rights Management, UNIAO BRASILEIRA DE EDITORAS DE MUSICA - UBEM, Sony ATV Publishing, CMRRA, LatinAutorPerf, and 10 Music Rights Societies

   Rachel Platten - Fight Song Fight Song EP is now available on iTunes! Download it here: http://smarturl.it/FightSongEP Follow Rachel Platten: Twitter: https://twitter.com/RachelPlatten Instagram: http://instagram.com/rachelplatten Facebook: https://www.facebook.com/rachelplatte... Tumblr: http://rachelplatten.tumblr.com/ We Heart It: http://weheartit.com/RachelPlatten Music Video by Rachel Platten performing "Fight Song." (C) 2015 Columbia Records, A Division of Sony Music Entertainment.

2. **Artist**: KESHA **Song**: PRAYING
Listen to Kesha: https://kesha.lnk.to/listenYD
Subscribe to the official Kesha YouTube channel: https://kesha.lnk.to/subscribeYD

Watch more Kesha videos: https://kesha.lnk.to/listenYC/ youtube Follow Kesha:

Facebook: https://kesha.lnk.to/followFI

Instagram: https://kesha.lnk.to/followII

Twitter: https://kesha.lnk.to/followTI

Website: https://kesha.lnk.to/followWI

Spotify: https://kesha.lnk.to/followSI

YouTube: https://kesha.lnk.to/subscribeYD

3. **Originally published:** 1922

Author: Margery Williams

Illustrator: William Nicholson

Genre: Children's novel

Characters: Nursery Magic Fairy, Nana, Skin Horse, Boy, Velveteen Rabbit

Chapter 3 – Let Go of People Pleasing and Set Boundaries

1. Written in a letter from Flannery O'Connor to Betty Hester on September 6, 1955. Flannery O'Connor was an American novelistand short-story writer.

2. Quote by Georgia O'Keeffe. Georgia Totto O'Keeffe was an American artist. She was known for her paintings of enlarged flowers, New York skyscrapers, and New Mexico landscapes. O'Keeffe has been recognized as the "Mother of American Modernism"

Chapter 4 – Frame the Shame – Tell Someone Safe your Secrets

1. Department of Psychology University of Texas at Austin 1 University Station A8000 Austin, TX 78712 512-232-2781 E-mail address: Pennebaker@mail.utexas.edu Webpage: https:// liberalarts.utexas.edu/psychology/faculty/pennebak

Chapter 6 – Acknowledge The Grief

1. Quote by Maya Angelou. Maya Angelou was an American poet, memoirist, and civil rights activist. She published seven autobiographies, three books of essays, several books of poetry, and is credited with a list of plays, movies, and television shows spanning over 50 years. She received dozens of awards and more than 50 honorary degrees.

Chapter 7: Realize That you Have Purpose (And It's Never Too Late!)

1. Quote by Oscar Wilde. Oscar Fingal O'Flahertie Wills Wilde was an Irish poet and playwright. After writing in different forms throughout the 1880s, he became one of the most popular playwrights in London in the early 1890s.

2. Poetically translated to "golden joinery," **Kintsugi**, or *Kintsukuroi,* is the centuries-old Japanese art of fixing broken pottery. Rather than rejoin ceramic pieces with a camouflaged adhesive, the Kintsugi technique employs a special tree sap lacquer dusted with powdered gold, silver, or platinum. Once completed, beautiful seams of gold glint in the conspicuous cracks of ceramic wares, giving a one-of-a-kind appearance to each "repaired" piece.

   This unique method celebrates each artifact's unique history by emphasizing its fractures and breaks instead of hiding or disguisingthem. In fact, Kintsugi often makes the repaired piece even more beautiful than the original, revitalizing it with a new look and giving it a second life.

3. Quote by Henri Nouwen. Henri Jozef Machiel Nouwen was a DutchCatholic priest, professor, writer and theologian. His interests were rooted primarily in psychology, pastoral ministry, spirituality, socialjustice and community.

If you received value from reading this book please go to Amazon and write a review.

You may also be interested in my online courses.

Learn more at
www.cindyjessecourses.com

www.ingramcontent.com/pod-product-compliance
Lightning Source LLC
LaVergne TN
LVHW021503080426
835509LV00018B/2381

* 9 7 8 1 7 3 6 4 2 3 5 4 *